👁 **INSIGHT** **POCKET GUIDE**

MOROCCO

GW00367409

Discovery CHANNEL

APA PUBLICATIONS
Part of the Langenscheidt Publishing Group

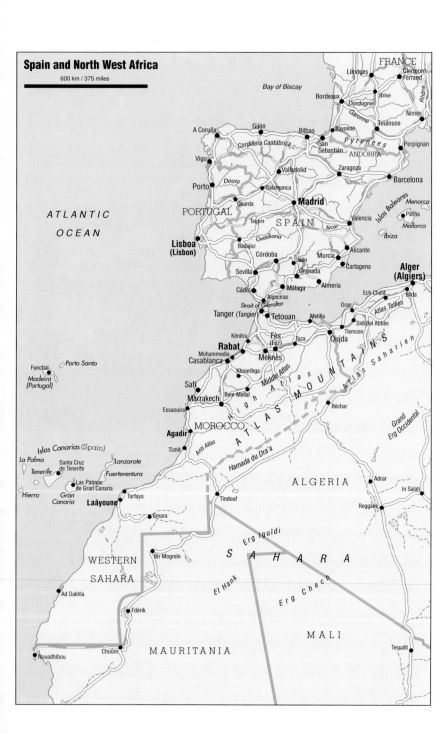

Spain and North West Africa

600 km / 375 miles

Welcome

This guidebook combines the interests and enthusiasms of two of the world's best-known information providers: Insight Guides, who have set the standard for visual travel guides since 1970, and Discovery Channel, the world's premier source of non-fiction television programming. Its aim is to help you get the most out of Morocco with the help of 13 itineraries devised by Dorothy Stannard, Insight's expert on North Africa.

Focusing on five key bases – Tangier, Rabat, Fez, Marrakesh and Agadir – the author has linked the highlights of each city in easy to follow walking tours and then devised excursions by car or public transport to other interesting towns and villages within easy reach, including trips through the Atlas Mountains to the south, an excursion to the fortified coastal town of Essaouira and a trip to Chaouen in the Rif Mountains. Each itinerary includes step-by-step directions – so that even when street signs are absent or in Arabic you still won't get lost – and ideas on where to eat, drink and relax on the way.

Supporting the itineraries are sections on history and culture, eating out, shopping, nightlife, festivals and a detailed practical information section containing advice on everything from money matters and getting around to matters of etiquette. This section also includes a list of hand-picked hotels, many of which the author has stayed in herself. In the wallet at the back of the guide is a large pullout map of the country plus detailed town plans of Tangier, Casablanca, Marrakesh, Fez and Rabat.

Dorothy Stannard first visited Morocco in the 1980s, lured there as a backpacker travelling with a friend. The relationships that were forged during that first visit led to countless returns since. Her advice to first-time visitors is this: 'Morocco isn't always an easy country to negotiate, for something of the old *bled es siba* (land of lawlessness) anarchy still prevails, but those who decide to go with the flow rather than fight it are rewarded by astonishing beauty, culture and encounters.'

HISTORY AND CULTURE

From Moulay Idriss I to Mohammed VI, from Berber and Arab dynasties to the French and Spanish Protectorates – an introduction to Morocco's history and culture.......**11**

ITINERARIES

The following itineraries concentrate on the highlights of Morocco. They are divided into five key areas – Tangier; Rabat & Casablanca; Fez & Meknes; Marrakesh; and Agadir & the Souss.

TANGIER

RABAT & CASABLANCA

FEZ & MEKNES

MARRAKESH

Pages 2–3: mountains meet the desert, the High Atlas
Pages 8–9: Taourirt Kasbah, near Ouarzazate

History *&Culture*

Crossing the Strait of Gibraltar to Morocco is one of the most dramatic short journeys a traveller can make. Europe is still in sight a hazy 14 km (9 miles) away yet suddenly one is immersed in an exotic brew of Arabia and Africa and pitched into a time warp that is a mind-bending fusion of the 1970s and the Middle Ages. On Tangier's Boulevard Pasteur elegantly coiffeured townswomen jostle with Jibali tribeswomen done up in red and white striped *ftouh* (wraps), bath towels, massive silver brooches and sombreros.

Berber Blood

The indigenous inhabitants of Morocco, indeed the whole of northwest Africa, are the Berbers, a mysterious tribal people whose origins have stumped ethnologists. There are three broad divisions, each with its own dialect, and numerous sub-divisions: the Riffians of the north, the Chleuhs of the Middle and High Atlas and the Soussi of the southwest.

When the Arabs swept westwards in the 7th century to spread the divine revelations entrusted to the Prophet Mohammed, the Berbers voluntarily embraced Islam, becoming fanatical adherents (though they retained elements of pagan pantheism, still evident today in rural areas). Indeed it was the Berbers who led the Muslim invasion of Spain in the 8th century; impelled to spread the faith *besiff* (by the sword), they routed the Visigoths and initiated seven centuries of brilliant civilisation at a time when the rest of Europe was still in the Dark Ages.

In secular matters, however, the Berbers remained implacable. Just as they had earlier chafed at Roman rule, they defied the distant Arab caliphate, revolting against the heavy taxes it imposed. Thus when, in 788, following Islam's split into Sunni and Shia sects, Idriss (grandson of the Prophet via the line of Ali) was exiled by the Sunni Abbasid caliphate, he found a welcome in Morocco's Volubilis. He founded Morocco's first independent Muslim dynasty, which could cock a snook at Baghdad.

Idriss's son, Idriss II, born to his father's Berber concubine, founded Fez. The city was augmented by waves of Shia refugees fleeing Córdoba (Spain) and Kairouan (Tunisia), the jewels of Western Islam, and Fez began to emerge as a centre of learning, trade (salt, gold, spices) and crafts. In 850 Kairouyine University was founded – one of the first universities in the world.

The following centuries brought other migrants to Morocco: troublesome tribes expelled from Arabia, Jews and Muslims fleeing the Inquisition in Spain and black Africans brought here as slaves from the Sahara.

With greater intermarriage between Berbers and Arabs, rural Moroccans in general became known for their rebellious nature.

Left: Delacroix painting of a sultan outside Meknes
Right: inspired by the Roman outpost of Volubilis

The areas where the tendency was strongest, in the mountainous hinterland and south, was known as the *bled es siba* – 'the land of lawlessness' – while the more easily controlled cities and coastal areas were known as the *bled el makhzan*, or 'land of the government'.

The resistance of the *bled es siba* is the main reason why Morocco didn't nudge its way into the modern age until the occupation of the French and Spanish. Turkish influences, so apparent in the rest of North Africa, are absent here, for the Ottomans never managed to penetrate *El Magreb el Aksa* (the land farthest west).

Historically the extent to which a sultan subdued the *bled es siba* determined his success. A series of weak sultans spelt decline for a dynasty, for there was always a more powerful tribe waiting in the wings. News of the untimely death of a sultan was kept quiet until a successor could be proclaimed. When Moulay Hassan (sultan 1873–94), for example, died in the *bled es siba* on the way back to Fez after a military campaign in the south, the information was kept secret for days, for fear of tribal revolt. In spite of the tell-tale stench from the palanquin, it was pretended that His Majesty was merely tired.

Challenges to the throne invariably came from the south – witness all

the major dynasties – the theory being that a dynasty grew decadent in the comfortable cities of the plains and coast, especially after contact with El Andalus (Muslim Spain). But for Abdelaziz (sultan 1894–1907), the threat came not from the Sahara but from Europe. Young and surrounded by fawning ministers, Abdelaziz bankrupted the country with a massive spending spree. The arrival in Morocco of a hansom cab and a gilded state coach, even though there were no roads, was marginally less ludicrous than the German motor-boat with its own German engineer, kept in a room in the royal palace, and a $40,000 British bulldog with false teeth sold to the sultan by an American con-man.

Consequently in 'the last scramble for Africa' at the beginning of the 20th century Morocco, an independent Muslim nation for over 1,000 years, lay vulnerable.

Top: *Religious Fanatics in Tangier* by Eugène Delacroix. **Left:** a Moroccan emir

French loans to stem the haemorrhage in the treasury accelerated European encroachment and, with the signing of the Treaty of Fez in 1912, Morocco was made a protectorate of France and Spain (the old border posts marking their zones of influence still stand just outside Arbaoua on the Tangier–Rabat road and on roads through the Rif). Tangier, considered crucial to Great Britain, which needed a friendly base close to Gibraltar, was designated an international zone. In theory the sultan was still pre-eminent; in reality, however, he was the puppet of colonial powers.

Occupation and its Legacy

European takeover of Morocco was not without bloodshed, and it was not until 1934 that France was able to pacify the whole of its zone, and then only thanks to a pact with Thami and Madani el Glaoui, tribal chiefs from the Atlas. Colonialism had its benefits, however. Roads, ports and railways were built and mining and farming developed, particularly in French Morocco. To begin with there were elements of idealism in French policy, personified by the first French Resident-General, Marshal Lyautey. He took pains to preserve Moroccan culture, building new towns well outside the traditional medinas, a policy that initially led to the isolation of the native community but which in the long term ensured the survival of Morocco's unique heritage.

French influence remains strong today. Casablanca likes to emulate Paris (though it is more like Marseille) and many aspects of life, from fashion to bureaucracy, take their cue from France. That children are now taught all lessons in Arabic rather than French is a relatively recent development, one likely to reduce the bilingualism (multilingualism for those who also speak Berber, Spanish or English) that is taken for granted among the educated population. French goods, cars in particular, are bought enthusiastically. Every summer thousands of Moroccan immigrants living in France (and also Belgium and Norway) embark on a long drive south for their annual month back home.

Notwithstanding the Spanish enclaves of Ceuta and Melilla, links with Spain are less pronounced (though proposals for a bridge across the Strait of Gibraltar occasionally surface). But vestiges of Spanish culture – architecture, *tapas*, disused bullrings and language – are found in northern towns such as Tetouan, Asilah and Larache, as is a Spanish timetable – late nights and a sluggish morning start.

In recent years increased emphasis on promoting indigenous culture has paid particular attention to the Berber languages. Television news is now broadcast in the three main Berber dialects at certain times of the day.

Right: Abdelaziz (sultan 1873–94) bankrupted Morocco

From Independence to Hassan

Morocco achieved independence in 1956, when nationalists, spearheaded by Istiqlal (Independence Party), could no longer be contained. The sultan, Sidi Mohammed ben Youssef, whose non-cooperation with the French had led to his exile in Madagascar, was flown home. On regaining the throne he changed his title to King Mohammed V to symbolise the dawn of a new age.

Tangier remained international for a few months longer. The city had flourished on the back of its free-port status, attracting profiteers as well as writers and artists such as Gertrude Stein and Matisse. The dismantling of the city's special status prompted a flurry of exits; but many Europeans in the city sat tight. In the event, Tangier continued to attract artists, bohemians and deviants, many of whom gravitated there on account of its reputation as a homosexual playground or for the ready availability of *kif* (hashish). The British journalist and author Kenneth Allsop wrote in the *Daily Mail* in 1959: 'The indigenous Tangier aroma, compounded of flowers, spices, hashish and Arab drains, is infiltrated by the pungent smell of typewriter ribbons from the overheated portables of best-selling London and New York novelists.'

The Reign of King Hassan II

Mohammed V died in 1961 and was succeeded by Hassan II. Reflecting on his succession with King Juan Carlos II of Spain 25 years later, he said: 'When I ascended the throne, people said I would not last more than six months.' He was referring to the surge of unrest unleashed by independence. The Istiqlal Party split into two factions, one of which, led by Mehdi ben Barka, had republican leanings.

Such treason was dealt with ruthlessly;

Above: Mohammed V returns from exile
Left: the writer William Burroughs in Tangier

Barka was assasinated in Paris and a state of emergency declared. This was later relaxed but the king retained his extensive powers, resulting in a couple of aborted army coups in the 1970s, when a combination of drought, excessive public spending, the plummeting price of phosphate (Morocco's chief export) and debt jeopardised stability.

But Hassan II had a powerful weapon – his descent from the Prophet Mohammed. Moroccans are at once devoutly Muslim and chronically superstitious, and descendants of the Prophet are held to have *baraka*, divine protection. To many, Hassan's escape from assassins at his 42nd birthday party in 1971, when nearly 100 of his guests were gunned down by 1,400 cadets (Hassan hid in a bathroom) was dramatic proof of divine intervention.

In the end, attention was diverted away from internal problems by the spectacular Green March of 6 November 1975, when 350,000 Moroccans, armed only with flags and copies of the Koran, marched into the Spanish Sahara (now known as the Western Sahara). They camped for three days under the guns of the Spanish Foreign Legion (which held fire), and then returned. Spain, preoccupied by the imminent death of Franco and keen to be rid of its desert colony, transferred administration of the territory to Morocco and Mauritania.

But then Algeria intervened, training and arming the Polisario, a group of left-wing guerrillas campaigning for the independence of the former Spanish colony. Whatever Algeria's real aims (perhaps to undermine King Hassan or secure access to the Atlantic), it cloaked them in the rhetoric of self-determination. Relations between Morocco and Algeria deteriorated to the point where, in 1981, Morocco began building defence lines along its border.

Contrary to Algeria's predictions, the problems of the Spanish Sahara strengthened rather than destabilised King Hassan and, by the end of the 1980s, Algeria was looking for a settlement. In 1988 Morocco and the Polisario accepted a United Nations peace plan: a ceasefire followed by a referendum among the people of the disputed territory.

Since then repeated attempts at a referendum have failed; the first, in January 1992, was postponed due to UN and Polisario disquiet at the Moroccan government moving 37,000 Moroccans into the Western Sahara on the grounds that their families had originated in the area.

While the UN Security Council rethinks its guidelines for the stalled referendum, UN peace-keeping forces sweat it out in the desert, threatening to withdraw if a solution cannot be found soon (the cost of deploying UN forces in the area is estimated to be around £2.4 million a month). Meanwhile the anniversary of the Green March (6 November) has become a national holiday, and maps of Morocco that don't include the Western Sahara are liable to be confiscated by the police.

Right: King Hassan II
Over Page: mothers and sons, Marrakesh

The Modern State

Modern Morocco is beset by problems – chronic unemployment, an escalating population (now nearly 29 million) and mushrooming shanty towns – yet King Hassan's reign went from strength to strength. Astute, pragmatic, sometimes ruthless, and just plain lucky, he managed to foster useful relations with Europe, the US and the Gulf States, clamp down on Islamic fundamentalists (while at the same time encouraging a popular reaffirmation of faith), as well as find time to develop a mean game of golf.

In 1993 the Hassan II Mosque opened in Casablanca. Built to mark Hassan's 60th birthday in 1989, it is an impressive monument to his reign, the tallest religious building in the world and on three sides flanked by the sea. In spite of arguments that the $600 million cost could have been spent more usefully, most Moroccans are proud of the magnificent mosque.

The Succession of Mohammed VI

In July 1999 Hassan II died after a bout of pneumonia. It was an event long dreaded by the people, who couldn't imagine life without their strong, autocratic king. But even before Hassan's death, there were indications that new, more liberal winds were blowing through the kingdom, and his 36-year-old son, King Mohammed VI, quickly captured the hearts and minds of most of his subjects by proposing a raft of reforms. Mohammed was reported as saying he wanted to rule over a state of law not of fear. One of his most significant acts was to sack Driss Basri, the country's much hated interior minister, who had run the security forces for 20 years and was known for his brutal suppression of human rights. At the same time, many political prisoners were released from jail and exiles were invited to return home.

As an absolute monarchy, Morocco reflects the personality of the king. Tradition and modernity comfortably coexist, a relationship mirrored by the twin halves of every city: the medina and the *nouvelle ville*. But the monarchy reflects Morocco too. Unlike some other Muslim countries, Morocco has never imposed progress at the expense of tradition. Scratch even the newest surface of this ancient kingdom and you will find the astonishing world of Sheherazade, where strange deeds and magic prevail and the Evil Eye is judged more powerful than a cruise missile.

HISTORY HIGHLIGHTS

12th century BC Phoenician sailors establish a series of trading posts along Morocco's coast.

146AD Carthage falls to Rome. Roman influence spreads west through North Africa. Volubilis, near modern-day Meknes, later becomes the capital of the Roman province of Mauritania Tingitana.

682 First Arab raids under the command of Oqba Ibn Nafi.

714 Further Arab incursions into Morocco and Spain. Berbers embrace Islam and invade Spain under Arab leadership.

788 Idriss I, exiled from Baghdad, is welcomed by Berber tribes in Volubilis and establishes Morocco's first Arab dynasty.

807 Idriss II founds Fez. Shortly after, Muslim refugees arrive from Andalusia in Spain and Kairouan, Tunisia.

1060–1147 The Almoravide dynasty sweeps up from the south as far as Spain. Founding of Marrakesh.

1147–1248 The Almohad dynasty. At its peak, their empire stretches from Spain to Tripoli. They build the Giralda in Seville, the Koutoubia in Marrakesh and the Tour Hassan in Rabat.

1248–1465 The Merenid dynasty. They build a chain of Islamic colleges and the Chellah necropolis in Rabat. Muslim and Jewish refugees arrive, fleeing the Inquisition in Spain. Portuguese and Spanish forces encroach on coastal cities.

1492 Fall of Muslim Spain.

1554–1669 The Saadian dynasty drives out the Christians. They build the Saadian tombs and El Badi Palace in Marrakesh. Ahmed el Mansour leads a gold rush to Timbuktu.

1669 Beginning of the present Alaouite dynasty.

1672–1727 Brutal but effective rule under Moulay Ismail in Meknes.

1894–1908 Sultan Abdelaziz leaves Morocco bankrupt and wide open to European encroachment.

1912 The Treaty of Fez. Morocco is carved up between France (which gets the lion's share) and Spain. Tangier becomes international.

1920s Thami el Glaoui, Pasha of Marrakesh, connives with the French, pacifying rebellious tribes in exchange for power and privileges.

1930–40s An independence movement centring on the Istiqlal Party emerges in Fez. Growing unrest is met by repression. Tangier's international set continues to swing.

1956 France grants Independence. Mohammed V changes the title sultan to King.

1961 Accession of Hassan II.

1963–77 King Hassan survives five different plots against him, the most serious of which are led by the army.

1975 The Green March. 350,000 unarmed Moroccans claim the Spanish (Western) Sahara for Morocco.

1976 The Polisario, aided by Algeria, disputes Morocco's claims on the Western Sahara.

1988 A referendum is promised to determine the fate of the Western Sahara. However, this is repeatedly postponed through the 1990s.

1993 The Hassan II Mosque opens in Casablanca.

1997 Increased democratisation leads to parliamentary elections and a narrow majority for the Socialist Union of Popular Forces (USAP). Abderrahmane Youssoufi is nominated as prime minister after more than 40 years in opposition.

1999 Hassan II dies. He is succeeded by his son, Mohammed VI.

2000–2002 Oil deposits are discovered in Eastern Morocco and also in waters off the Western Sahara.

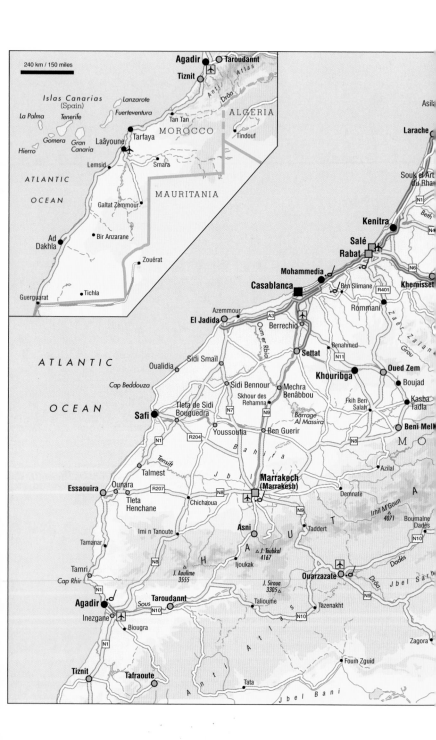

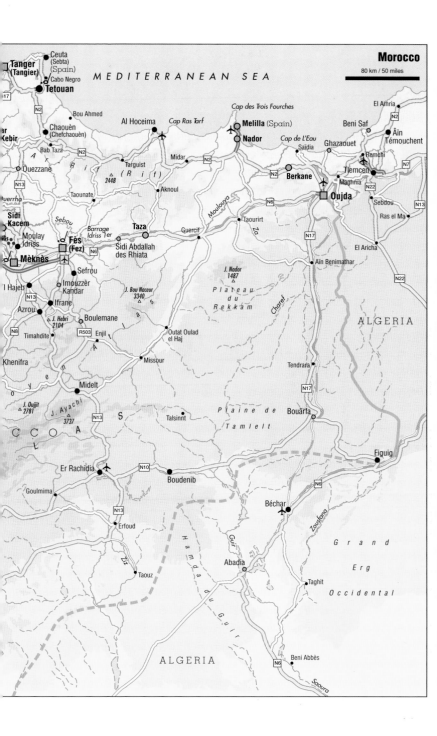

MEDITERRANEAN SEA

Morocco

80 km / 50 miles

Tanger
(Tangier)

Ceuta
(Sebta)
(Spain)

Cabo Negro

Tetouan

El Amria

17

N2

Bou Ahmed

Cap des Trois Fourches

Cap des Trois Fourches

Chaouèn
(Chefchaouèn)

Al Hoceima

Cap Ras Tarf

Melilla (Spain)

Beni Saf

Âïn
Témouchent

N2

r
Kebir

Bab Taza

N2

Nador

Cap de L'Eau

Saïdia

Ghazaouet

Quezzane

Targuist

Midar

N2

Za

Berkane

Remchi

Tlemcen

N7

N13

R i f
(R i f)

2448

Taounate

Aknoul

N2

N6

Maghnia

N22

Oujda

Sebdou

N13

uerrha

Sidi
Kacem

Sebou

Barrage
Idriss 1er

Taza

Guercif

Taourirt

Ras el Ma

ris

Moulay
Idriss

Fès
(Fez)

Sidi Abdallah
des Rhiata

El Aricha

Mèknès

N6

Aïn Benimathar

N22

l Hajeb

Sefrou

J. Nador
1487

Imouzzèr
Kandar

J. Bou Naceur
3340

P l a t e a u
d u
R e k k a m

Charef

ALGERIA

Azrou

Ifrane

S

J. Hebri
2104

Boulemane

a

N8

Timahdite

R503

Enjil

Outat Oulad
el Haj

A

Khenifra

e
n

Missour

Tendrara

N17

Midelt

J. Oujjit
2781

J. Ayachi
3737

N13

S

Plaine de

Bouârfa

o

Talsinnt

Tamlelt

C C O

A

Figuig

L

Er Rachidia

N10

Boudenib

N6

Goulmima

Béchar

Zousfana

N13

Erfoud

Ziz

Hamda du Guir

Guir

G r a n d

Taouz

Abadia

E r g

Taghit

O c c i d e n t a l

ALGERIA

N6

Beni Abbès

Saoura

tangier

Tangier

Few places of its size have such a colourful past as Tangier. At its peak as an international zone in the 1940s and '50s it drew a rich mix of spies, smugglers, homosexuals, writers and world-famous stars. While Tennessee Williams and Allen Ginsberg sipped mint tea in Tangier's Petit Socco, the Woolworth heiress Barbara Hutton shared nuptial bliss with her third husband, Cary Grant, in her palatial villa in the Kasbah.

Following independence, both the sleaze and the glamour waned. Nowadays only vestiges remain: the town is still something of a mecca among older gays; there is a cliquey expatriate community; and until his death in 1999 Paul Bowles presided over a rather leaner literary set. But it is no longer 'Interzone', the nightmarish place that William Burroughs portrayed in his novel *The Naked Lunch* which was inspired by and set in Tangier. Indeed, Cecil Beaton's description of 'an oriental Cheltenham' seems more apt.

But Tangerinos, the Europeans in Tangier, are only part of the story. Native *Tanjawis* are looking to their future rather than the past. The city is spreading in all directions, and property prices are rocketing. Long ignored by Hassan II, the city has received several visits from Mohammed VI, whose palace is on the northwest side of town, and a new duty-free port is planned south of the city.

With its magnificent bay, Tangier is a popular tourist destination, not least among the Moroccans themselves, and in high summer you will find it bursting at the seams. To escape the crush, venture west to the quieter beaches of Cap Spartel or the long swathe of sand stretching 40km (25 miles) along the Atlantic seaboard to Asilah *(see page 26)*, fortified by the Portuguese in the 17th century. Now something of an artists' town, Asilah is known for its colourful murals, which are renewed for its excellent cultural festival in August. Also worth discovering are the quiet coves along the road to the Spanish enclave of Ceuta (Sebta), east of Tangier, in particular Ksar es Seghir, overlooking the mouth of a river, and 11km (7 miles) further on, the superb beach below the village of Dalia *(see page 27)*.

Getting Around

The centre of Tangier is small, so you can easily get around on foot. You will probably find *petit-taxis* useful in the evening or for getting to the bus, train and *servis* (shared taxi) stations (on the Tetouan road out of town). For trips out of town (tours 2 and 3, for example), a car is recommended (rental companies are found mainly off Boulevard Mohammed V), though Asilah and Chaouen can be reached by bus. Asilah is also on the railway running south to Rabat, but trains are infrequent and Asilah station is a long walk from the centre.

Left: carrying the shopping home in Tangier's medina
Right: baby carrier

1. THE TOWN AND THE BEACH *(see map below)*

A morning's walking tour of Tangier, beginning in the New Town and progressing to the medina and Kasbah. In the afternoon, sample the city beach or drive to the quieter coves of Cap Spartel.

Begin the day with a *café au lait* or a fresh orange juice at one of the cafés on Boulevard Pasteur. Manilla, about half way along on the sunny side of the street, is a good option. The cafés also serve croissants, *pain au chocolat*, and flat bread filled with a light creamy cheese. Boulevard Pasteur and its continuation, Boulevard Mohammed V, contain the main banks, the tourist office (29 Boulevard Pasteur), the post office (Mohammed V) and the Libraire des Colonnes (54 Boulevard Pasteur), a good bookshop. In the side streets running off Pasteur are many of the town's restaurants and bars.

Afterwards follow the boulevard north, passing a line of 19th-century cannons and views over the harbour, to the Place de France, overlooked by the French embassy. Here, the **Café de Paris**, with Art Deco flourishes still intact, was something of an institution in the international era. From here, Rue de la Liberté curls down to the Grand Socco, passing the five-star El Minzah Hotel, originally the private home of a rich American and later the Palmarium Casino, and on the left the Galerie Delacroix, a venue for temporary art exhibitions. The **Grand Socco** is a bustling square-cum-market whose name reflects the city's hybrid past. The **Mosque of Sidi Bouabid**, with its delicately tiled minaret, overlooks the Socco; it was the first mosque to be built outside the medina's walls.

Into the Medina

Cross the Socco and take the street to the right of the keyhole gate, **Rue Siaghine** (though you may also see plaques saying Rue Semmarine and even Rue des Postes, its former

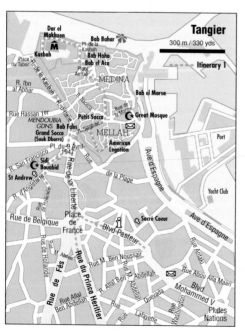

name). After 20 metres/yds or so it passes on the right a small entrance to the **market**, usually lined by *Jibali* women dressed in red and white *ftouh* (wraps) and staw hats, down from the hills to sell eggs, vegetables and crumbly curd cheeses. Take a look inside, if only to inhale the aromas and enjoy the larder-cool air.

A little way past the market (before No 79), strike right down Rue Touahine, the entrance to the old *mellah* (Jewish quarter), which is crammed with goldsmiths. At the end of the street turn right into Rue Kadi Temsamani, which bends round to the left. A few steps further on, turn

right into Rue d'Amerique, where you will find the **American Legation** (Mon–Fri 10am–1pm and 3–5pm or by appointment; tel: 039-935317; admission free; a knowledgeable guide conducts tours). Morocco was the first country to recognise American independence and the old legation was the first American government property outside the United States. It contains many fine oil paintings, watercolours, lithographs and photographs of Morocco, including work by Eugène Delacroix, the Scottish artist James McBey, who lived in Morocco, and contemporary Moroccan painters such as R'bati and Hamri. Among the archive materials on display, look out for letters from George Washington recording an agreement guaranteeing American immunity from Moroccan corsairs.

Retrace your steps to Rue Siaghine and carry on downhill to the **Petit Socco** (officially called Place Souk Dakhile), a triangular intersection that formed the hub of Tangier's notorious lowlife during the international era. Hundreds of illicit deals have been sealed on the terrace of Café Central. It was here that William Burroughs, nicknamed 'the invisible man' by the locals on account of his stick-like figure, found inspiration for *The Naked Lunch*. The place still has a slightly edgy feel.

As you hit the Petit Socco, take the first street on the left, Rue el Mouahidine (past Café Tingis), and run the gauntlet of souvenir bazaars to the end. Here turn left into Rue Sidi Ben Raissoul. After crossing a small *place* the street climbs up to the Kasbah, the stronghold of the town, passing after about five minutes Sidi Hosni, a home of the Woolworth heiress Barbara Hutton from 1946 until her death in 1979. Opposite the house, tucked around the corner, is the entrance to the Ali Baba café (identified by the psychedelic mural on its wall), a good place for a drink and views over Sidi Hosni's terrace, where Hutton devised extravagant parties for rich and famous guests. She reputedly had certain streets in the Kasbah widened to accommodate her Rolls-Royce. In 2002 Sidi Hosni was put on the market for $2.5 million – a snip in European terms but a fortune by local standards.

The Kasbah

From here, continue to Place Amrah and pass through a gate to Place de la Kasbah. **Bab Bahar** (the sea gate), overlooking the bay, is to the right, behind a corner of the *place* traditionally reserved for the punishment of female miscreants; to the left and then tucked up to the right, past the old prison and treasury,

Above: Jibali tribeswomen come to Tangier to trade
Right: the Kasbah Museum

is the **Dar el Makhzen**, the former palace of the governor and used in 1912 by the abdicate Sultan Moulay Hafid. Now a **museum** (Sat–Mon, Wed and Thur 9am–12.30pm and 3–5.30pm, Fri 9–11.30am; admission charge), it is an attractive setting for armour, wedding and circumcision costumes, ceramics, carpets, furniture and Roman finds from Cotta on Cap Spartel.

At the exit from the palace gardens turn left into Rue Riad Sultan which leads to Place du Tabor. Proceed through the gate on its far side and turn left down Rue de la Kasbah, which becomes Rue d'Italie at Hamadi's Restaurant. A left turn into the medina opposite Café Excelsior leads to the supposed **tomb of Ibn Battouta**, a famous 14th-century geographer and traveller who was born in Tangier. Non-Muslims are usually allowed to view the tomb.

Rue d'Italie leads back to the Grand Socco via the keyhole arch. Cross the Socco and take Rue d'Angleterre to the Anglican church of **St Andrew's**, whose English interior is successfully enlivened by North African embellishments. Moustafa, the church's caretaker, will point out several interesting tombstones, including the grave of Walter Harris, a 19th-century correspondent for the London *Times* and the author of *Morocco that Was*, a classic work on Morocco.

Emerging from the churchyard, take Rue de Hollande uphill. Opposite the derelict Grand Hôtel Villa de France, where Henri Matisse stayed and painted on two fruitful visits to Tangier in 1912 and 1913, is **Dawliz**, a restaurant and cinema complex (showing recent Hollywood hits, French films and critically acclaimed Arab films, usually with French subtitling). Its upstairs café has a panoramic view of the town, medina, kasbah and port from its terrace.

Cap Spartel

In the afternoon those without their own transport could do worse than lounge around on the city's beach. If the pesky east wind *(chergui)* is blowing, make use of one of the many beach clubs. Each of these has its own character (Emma's BBC and Chellah are reliable choices), providing sunbeds, sheltered terrace, shower and changing facilities, snacks and a bar.

Around Tangier

Those with their own transport may prefer to head for **Cap Spartel** via the 'mountain road' (follow signs for Montagne), passing on the way Tangier's most exclusive properties, including the royal palace and a palace belonging to King Fahd of Saudi Arabia.

The best of the cape's small sandy coves lie beyond (in an anticlockwise direction) the turning for the cape's lighthouse (in itself not particularly worth visiting, though

there are camel rides, a café and a few souvenir stands). After a refreshing swim, you can watch the sun go down over a mint tea on the terrace of one of the makeshift summer cafés that spring up along the bays or, if you would prefer a beer, at **Robinson's Hotel** further on. Close to the hotel are the **Caves of Hercules** (9am–sunset; tip for guide), which, in the 1950s and '60s, were used for parties, including one hosted by Cecil Beaton.

From the caves, continue to follow the road round, passing the sparse ruins of Roman **Cotta**, next to which is the surface terminal for a new US$3.5 billion pipeline taking natural gas from Algeria to Europe. A turning left before the road joins the main Tangier–Rabat road leads back to Tangier via the city prison. If you are hungry and want to dine simply but well, a petrol station on the left just past the prison has a garden grill restaurant. Popular with locals, it serves excellent and inexpensive *harira*, kebabs and salad.

A Night on the Town

Tangier has several good restaurants in the centre of town *(see Eating Out, page 81)*. *Tanjawis* tend to dine late (around 10pm), but most places will be open from around 7pm.

After dinner, explore the city's bars – try the **Tanger Inn** (on Rue Magellan), **Casa Ocaña** (Rue Rembrandt), **Chico's** and **The Pub** (both Rue Sorolla) or the convivial **Caïd's Bar** in El Minzah Hotel, Rue de la Liberté. To cap your evening, you could visit the **Morocco Palace**, Rue Abdel ben Abdallah, which offers kitsch Moroccan decor, musicians and hostesses (the promise of belly-dancing isn't delivered until around 1am, when things hot up) or **Pasarela**, on Avenue des FAR running alongside the beach.

Above: the lighthouse at Cap Spartel
Right: Caves of Hercules, Cap Spartel

2. TO ASILAH
(see map, p24)

**A drive south of Tangier to the for-
tified town of Asilah, 40km (26
miles) from Tangier, for a look at
the pretty medina, a walk along the
ramparts, and a fish lunch. Asilah
is an attractive destination at any
time of the year, but it is particularly worth visiting during the
town's arts festival in August.**

*This excursion is best by car. However,
buses and shared taxis for Asilah, leaving from the main bus station at Jama
el-Arabia (on the Tetouan road about
2km/1 mile from the centre of Tangier
– take a petit-taxi to get there) are fairly
regular. The train is not really recommended, as trains are infrequent and
Asilah station is a long (and in summer hot) walk from the town.*

The drive to Asilah along the main N1 Tangier to Rabat road takes about
30 minutes. The route, which is usually busy, follows the Atlantic seaboard,
allowing some excellent views of the impressively long and sandy beach that
runs all the way. There are few landmarks on the route; after Gzanaia the road
passes the Diplomatic Forest, a favourite picnic spot, especially on the 1 May
holiday, and an American military base, identified by its forest of radio
transmitters.

One in a string of similar coastal towns captured and fortified by the Portuguese in the 15th and 16th centuries (others include Larache, El Jadida and
Essaouira), Asilah is an attractive whitewashed town, with bright blue doors,

windows covered in Andalusian grillework,
and streets and squares lined with bushy citrus trees. Like Essaouira further south, it has
become a magnet for musicians and artists.
In August, prior to its international arts festival, the medina walls are covered in abstract
murals. Its beach, to the north of town, is
broad and sandy, but without shade and with
a busy road and the railway running alongside. There are several small hotels in town,
and camping/holiday club complexes can
be found on the outskirts.

Bab el Kasaba
Arriving in Asilah, head for Place Zellaca,
on which the fine Bab el Kasaba leads into
the medina (parking can be found around
here, but be careful, as many of the curbs

Above: the ramparts, Asilah
Left: a fine catch, Asilah

are painted with red and white stripes indicating no-parking). Walk through the gate and follow the main drag, which leads to the ramparts built by the Portuguese in 1471. Along the way, notice the palace (a main venue for performances during the August festival) built in 1909 by Shereef Ahmed el Raisuli, a self-styled ruler who was credited with considerable *baraka* (spiritual power) by the *Jibali* tribespeople living around Tangier. Raisuli kidnapped a number of high-profile westerners, including Walter Harris, the correspondent of the London *Times*. Nonetheless he was made governor of the region by Sultan Moulay Abdelaziz in 1909 and remained so under the Spanish, who clearly considered it better to have him as an ally rather than an enemy. Raisuli rebelled against the Spanish on several occasions.

Back on Place Zellaca, walk around towards the corniche, where a number of fish restaurants (all licensed) offer good-value fish and seafood. Particularly recommended are **Casa Garcia**, on the corniche opposite the new, rather sparse marina, or (slightly cheaper) **Casa Pepe**, with pavement tables overlooking the main gate to the medina. Aim to have lunch by 2pm at the latest, as they tend to close from around 2.30 or 3pm until dinner.

3. CHAOUEN   *(see map, p24)*

A two-day excursion (also possible in one long day) to the refreshing mountain town of Chaouen (Chefchaouen) via the Mediterranean coast to Ksar es Seghir and Tetouan.

Chaouen has plenty of hotels, but one of the best options is the Parador (pool, views, restaurant; tel: 039-986324), at the top of the town beyond Plaza Uta el Hamman.

This tour into the foothills of the Rif is especially recommended in summer, when the cooler air of Chaouen is reviving. It travels through pretty scenery, dotted with *Jibali* tribeswomen, distinctive in their red and white *ftouh* and sombrero-style hats, selling cheeses, walnuts, strawberries, lychees or whatever is in season.

If you are spreading this tour over two days, take the chance to explore the small bays east of Tangier on the way. Take the much improved road to the Spanish enclave of Ceuta (signposted Sebta), leaving Tangier via Avenue d'Espagne, running alongside the beach. The route runs past several attractive beaches, including Plage des Amiraux (signposted) just a few kilometres from Tangier. At **Ksar es Seghir** (28km/17 miles from Tangier) the road to Chaouen (Chefchaouen) leads inland via Tetouan, but if you fancy spending an hour or so on one of the loveliest beaches in the north, first drive 11km (7 miles) on to **Dalia**, turning left down a track below the village (immediately after a large rocky outcrop

Right: into the medina, Chaouen

on the left of the road). Backed by an amphitheatre of pine trees, this arc of white sand lapped by crystal-clear waters has become a popular spot for summer campers, but out of season you will probably find it deserted.

Afterwards, return to Ksar es Seghir, where the first-floor balcony tables of the restaurant **Laachari** (unlicensed) overlooks the river and fort. Its good-value fish and seafood often attract Spanish parties, who drive over from Ceuta.

From Ksar es Seghir, take the road south to **Tetouan**, the former capital of the Spanish protectorate, as reflected in the imposing Spanish-style buildings. The town does a roaring trade in tax-free goods smuggled from the Spanish enclave of Ceuta, and has some of the best souks in the north, spreading back from Bab el Rouah (Gate of the Winds), off the central Place Hassan II, the site of the Royal Palace. From Tetouan the road heads through the foothills of the Rif, brushing the *kif*-growing region radiating from Ketama. Despite the Moroccan government's attempts to clamp down on the *kif*/hashish trade in this region, Morocco is still the world's largest exporter of hashish.

Mountain Idyll

After a further 57km (37 miles) **Chaouen** (also written Chefchaouen) appears in the spur of the hills. Its higgledy-piggledy medina is enchanting. Look for clues to medina life: hand and fish motifs on the buildings, to ward off the Evil Eye, stashes of wood to feed the fires of the local baker or *hammam* (public baths), children on street corners spinning braid to decorate kaftans. The ubiquitous whitewash is often tinged with blue, a colour believed to deflect mosquitoes as well as the Evil Eye.

The picturesque centre is the **Plaza Uta el Hammam**, with its sandstone kasbah, citrus trees and cafés, where you can relax over a mint tea. The rest of the afternoon can be spent visiting the kasbah museum, shopping among the craft stalls or cooling down in the hotel pool. The next day, wind your way back to Tangier, taking the N2 from Tetouan, or drive on to Fez *(see page 35)*, a route with little traffic and exhilarating scenery.

Above: the stepped streets of Chaouen
Right: mosque on the Plaza Uta el Hammam

Rabat & Casablanca

Rabat seems peculiarly staid for a capital city. Activity quickly peters out away from the central spine, the Avenue Mohammed V, and even the medina, which is built on a grid system, seems sober compared with the old areas of Fez or Marrakesh. Rabat cleaves to the mouth of the river of Bou Regreg (Father of Reflection), directly opposite its twin and moral conscience, Salé, a 'dry' (no alcohol), culturally resolute town with a pious reputation.

The Almohad and Merenid remains that distinguish Rabat's centre are testimonies to its historical importance, but apart from brief periods during the 12th and 18th centuries the city didn't enjoy capital status until the French Protectorate. The name Rabat stems from *ribat*, the name given to the religious-cum-military communities that punctuated the North African coast between the 10th and 12th centuries to defend orthodox Islam against infidels and heretics. The one at Rabat was used first to subdue heretic Berber tribes and later to launch *jihads* (religious invasions) into Spain.

Rabat-Salé shot to European attention in the 17th century when it became the independent pirate republic of Bou Regreg (1627–41), formed by Andalusian refugees expelled from Spain by the Inquisition. With time on their hands and a desire for revenge, the Sallee Rovers, as they were known, plagued the North African coast, plundering European ships. It was the Sallee Rovers who captured Daniel Defoe's Robinson Crusoe off the Canary Islands. To this day Andalusian influences are clearly visible in the architecture of the Kasbah of the Oudayas above the medina.

4. CAPITAL CITY *(see map, p30)*

A day's walking tour linking the main sights, including the Mausoleum of Mohammed V, the Tour Hassan, the Kasbah of the Oudayas, the archaeological museum and the Chellah.

Visitors with more time may prefer to split this tour over two mornings, leaving the afternoons free for the beach west of the Kasbah (if you have transport, try Skhirate beach, near the Royal Palace 30km/19 miles south of Rabat) or a dip into Salé across the estuary (fishing boats ferry people across for a few dirhams).

The **Tour Hassan** (Hassan's Tower), the most important sight in Rabat and easily spotted on the generally low-rise skyline, makes a suitable starting point. The tower is the minaret of a great mosque planned by the Almohad

Right: Kasbah of the Oudayas rising above the river of Bou Regreg

Yacoub el Mansour in honour of victories in Spain at the end of the 12th century. It belongs to a trio of similar minarets designed by the same architect, the others being the Koutoubia in Marrakesh and the Giralda in Seville, the latter later topped by a Christian belfry. The Tour Hassan rises to only 50 metres (165ft) of its projected 81 metres (265ft). The mosque it was to serve, though also never finished, reached a more advanced stage than the evidence today suggests; the Lisbon earthquake of 1755 reduced the prayer hall, intended to contain 40,000 worshippers, to rows of stumpy pillars.

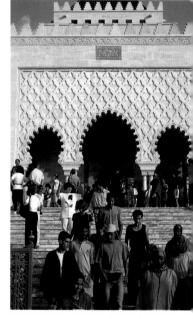

Situated south of the mosque is the white **Mausoleum of Mohammed V** (also open to non-Muslims), containing the tombs of Mohammed V (the large central one) and those of his two sons. To many people's surprise, Hassan II's tomb is very modest (the smallest of the three). Before his death in 1999, it had been assumed that Hassan would occupy the large adjoining mausoleum.

The Medina and Kasbah

Exit on the river side of the complex, walk through the park and proceed downhill. At Avenue Hassan II turn left, keeping the walls of the medina on your right. After 300 metres/yds, turn right into the medina onto Rue des Consuls, once the only street where foreign consuls and merchants could operate in the town. Today, it specialises in carpets on Tuesdays and Thursdays, when women come to sell their carpets directly, giving buyers the chance to cut out the middleman.

At the end of Rue des Consuls cross the road and climb the steps to the **Kasbah of the Oudayas**, built by Almohad Yacoub el Mansour on the site of the original *ribat*. This was the heart of the corsair republic in the 17th century. Take the first gate on the right into the **Andalusian Garden**, an enclosure of fruit trees, flowers

Above: Mausoleum of Mohammed V and Hassan II

and vines, formerly the sultan's gardens. The ticket office for an interesting **museum** (9am–noon and 3–5.30pm, closed Tues; admission charge) of regional costumes, jewellery, weaponry, carpets and musical instruments, occupying rooms of the former palace, is off to the left at the top of the garden. There is also a small art gallery on the right at the top of the garden, next to the entrance to Café Maure, a delightful blue and white café tucked into the battlements, offering good mint tea, pastries and ocean breezes and views.

Afterwards, return to the exterior of the kasbah and walk up to the main gate, now the entrance to another art gallery. Take the small gate to its right into the typically Andalusian Rue Jamaa. Follow this to the far corner of the Kasbah, from where there are more fine views.

Retracing your route, regain the Kasbah's exterior, but instead of returning to Rue des Consuls cross the road to the triangular Place l'Oudaya, the market for Christian captives during the Bou Regreg republic. From here, head along Boulevard el-Alou (running at right-angles to the Kasbah's walls), passing the wool market. Turn left at Avenue Mohammed V, which cuts through the medina to become the city's main boulevard shortly past the central market.

Avenue Mohammed V runs directly from the medina to the Great Mosque and the Royal Palace. About a third of the way along its length, at the intersection with Rue Halab, you can stop and have lunch at Café La Renaissance, an old-fashioned brasserie which serves basic fare and beers.

The Archaeological Museum

This afternoon's itinerary explores the other end of town. Suitably refreshed, continue along Mohammed V, passing the parliament building on the right and Hotel Balima, one-time recipient of visiting dignitaries, directly opposite. Just past the station, branch right up Avenue Moulay Youssef to reach **Bab er Rouah** (the Gate of the Winds), Rabat's only extant Almohad gate except the main entrance to the Kasbah. Temporary exhibitions are held inside. From the gate, walk along Avenue Moulay Hassan as if to return to Boulevard Mohammed V, but just past the Great Mosque branch right and first left (Rue Moulay Abdelaziz). At Hotel Chellah turn right into Rue Ali Brihi for the **Archaeological Museum** (8.30–11.30am and 2.30–5.30pm, closed Tues; admission charge).

The highlight of the museum is the **Salle de Bronzes** (separate entrance), containing a magnificent collection of bronzes recovered from Volubilis, including a superb head of Juba II of Mauritania Tingitania and an ivy-crowned youth (the *Ephebus*). The other rooms contain mainly material from Morocco's other archaeological sites, in particular Sala Colonia, the Roman forerunner of the Chellah *(see page 32)*.

Right: the Andalusian Garden in the Kasbah of the Oudayas

Note a stele inscribed with Latin on one side and Arabic on the other; Sala Colonia was one of the last towns to sever links with the Roman Empire.

The Chellah

To get to the **Chellah** (8.30am–half an hour before sunset; admission charge) from the museum, take Avenue Yacoub el Mansour (directly behind the Great Mosque). It is a 15-minute walk, so if it is hot and you are tired, hail a taxi. You will see the Chellah's walls when you emerge through Bab Zaer at the end of the street. Crumbling, semi-wild and colonised by storks, the Chellah is a royal burial ground which was built on the ruins of the Roman port of Sala Colonia in the 13th century. Engage the services of a guide to steer you through its overgrown paths. The royal tombs are behind the mosque and include the tomb of the power-ful Merenid sultan Abou el Hassan, known as the Black Sultan on account of his Abyssinian mother. Close to the mosque is a sunken pool inhabited by a colony of eels, sacred creatures said to confer fertility and fed with hard-boiled eggs by wistful women visitors. On leaving the Chellah, take a taxi back to your hotel.

Evenings in Rabat centre on the evening promenade along Avenue Mohammed V. The terrace of Hotel Balima is a lively spot to sit and watch; it is also within close proximity of La Mamma's (behind the hotel, in Zekat Tant), one of the best Italian restaurants-cum-pizzerias in Morocco and popular among well-heeled Rabatis. If you want something authentically Moroccan, you could take a taxi to Dinarjat in the medina or to the Moroc-can restaurant in La Tour Hassan Hotel.

5. EXCURSION TO CASABLANCA *(see map, p34)*

A morning trip to Casablanca, Morocco's largest city, for a guided tour (not conducted on Fridays) of the biggest mosque in Africa. Afterwards have lunch at one of Morocco's best fish restaurants at Aïn Diab, the coastal stretch west of the mosque.

Those without their own transport can get to Casablanca easily by train from Rabat Ville, on Avenue Mohammed V (in Casablanca get off at Casa Port station). Drivers have a choice of three clearly indicated roads from Rabat. During mid-week choose the coast road, which is marginally more pleasant than the motorway or the N1, but avoid this on summer weekends when it is ensnarled with beach-bound city dwellers. To take a guided tour of the Hassan II Mosque it is essential to dress respectably. If you want to have lunch at A ma Bretagne, you should book ahead (tel: 022-397979; closed Sun) but there are less expensive alternatives nearby.

Just 90km (56 miles) along the coast from Rabat, Casablanca inevitably beckons fans of one of the most romantic movies ever made. The real Casablanca, however, has little in common with the studio get-up of Sin City portrayed in the Bogart-Bergman film. Modern, noisy and Africa's second-largest city after Cairo, it is the closest Morocco comes to fast; indeed it feels a lot more like a capital than Rabat.

Providing you don't expect to find Rick's Café Americain, it makes an interesting half-day excursion, not least on account of its fine French and neo-Mauresque (circa1920s) architecture. Beginning at **Place Mohammed V** (formerly called Place des Nations Unies), a magnificent square adorned with shooting fountains and graced by four imposing neo-Mauresque buildings, walk down Avenue Hassan II to Place des Nations Unies (formerly Place Mohammed V), dominated by the Hyatt Regency hotel. From here, turn into Boulevard Mohammed V and dip into the pristine market a little way

along on the left-hand side. At Boulevard Hassan Seghir, turn left to reach Place Zellaga, then turn left into Avenue des FAR where you will see the sumptuous **Royal Mansour Hotel** on the right-hand side. The ground-floor atrium café-bar is a good place to have a morning coffee.

Carrying on along Avenue des FAR, you regain Place des Nations Unies. From here, you may want to drop into the medina for a look at Casa's more traditional side. In the morning and evening the streets turn into an open bazaar with piles of merchandise spilling over the streets. You might also take a look at activity in the **fishing port** at the end of Boulevard Mohammmed el Hansali.

Left: the Kasbah (top) and Chellah, Rabat.
Right: Hassan II Mosque, Casablanca

Hassan II Mosque

Afterwards, return to your car and drive, or take a taxi, along the corniche to Aïn Diab, passing on the way the **Hassan II Mosque**, financed by public 'contributions' (special officials collected donations from every home in the land) to mark King Hassan's 60th birthday in 1989. The mosque, inaugurated in 1993, is the largest in Africa and, with a minaret of 175 metres (575 ft) it is the tallest religious building in the world. Designed by the French architect Michel Pinseau, it was built at a cost of US$750 million. It has space for some 20,000 worshippers and an electronically operated sun-roof. It incorporates a library, museum, steam baths, Koranic school and conference facilities.

As far as possible it incorporates Moroccan materials, such as cedar from the Middle Atlas and marble from Agadir and Tafraoute. It took 35,000 workers 50 million man-hours to complete.

The mosque is the only active mosque in Morocco open to non-Muslims, but they can only enter by joining a guided tour (admission charge). These are conducted in French and start at 9am, 10am, 11pm and 2pm (2.30pm in summer), except Friday, when no tours take place. Even if you don't understand French, it is well worth taking the opportunity to get a close look at the work of Morocco's finest living craftsmen.

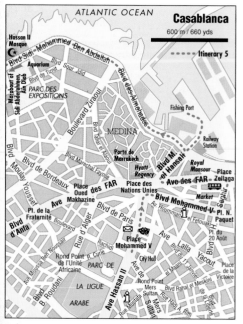

Aïn Diab

The coastal strip west of Casa, known as Aïn Diab, is the city's playground. But offshore at its far end, where the flashy restaurants, nightspots and beach clubs subside to urban wasteland and gaunt cranes, is a very different kind of attraction – the **marabout of Sidi Abderahmen**, a cluster of tombs and pilgrims' lodging-houses on a rocky outcrop rising out of the waves. The fish restaurant **A ma Bretagne** is 200m/yards further on. If you can't afford the steep prices, in summer there is a café in front of the marabout where you can order *brochettes* and tea and watch the pilgrims going to and fro.

Above Left: on the rocks, Aïn Diab

Fez & Meknes

O ld Fez, Fez el Bali, is a highlight of any trip to Morocco. One of the
world's last pockets of medieval civilisation, it is peppered with old
palaces and *madrassas* (Islamic colleges), their blank walls conceal-
ing intricate interiors, and packed with the still busy workshops of ancient
industries. The sounds and smells of this city stimulate and soothe in turn.

In 1976 Fez's old city was declared a World Heritage Site by UNESCO,
which in 1980 launched a programme of restoration (still in progress).
Whether the medina can withstand the pressures being placed on it by over-
population, dilapidation and pollution without being turned into a museum
is a subject of debate. Thirteenth-century sewers and clay piping struggle
to cope with the needs of 200,000 people.

Old Fez lies in an elongated trough of hills, and falls into two parts: Fez
el Bali (9th century), and Fez el Jdid (12th century). Fez el Bali itself divides
into the Andalous quarter on the east bank of the Oued Fes, settled by Arab
refugees from Andalusia in 818, and the Kairouyine quarter on the west
bank, settled by refugees from Kairouan, Tunisia, in 825. The Almoravide
and Almohad dynasties made Marrakesh their capital but Fez retained its reputation as Morocco's intellectual and religious centre. The Merenids re-
established the city's capital status and built Fez el Jdid.

Centuries later the French built the Nouvelle Ville, a couple of kilometres to the southwest, hooked up to the medina by Boulevard Moulay Youssef.
The New Town contains most of the city's hotels.

6. A DAY IN FEZ *(see map, p38)*

**First to a palatial museum, then a trip through time to Fez
el Bali, Fez's holy heart; lunch, the tanneries and mint tea
in the gardens of Palais Jamai.**

*If you plan to spend more than one day in Fez, it is better to split
this itinerary into two morning tours (having a buffet lunch instead
of tea at Palais Jamai on the second morning), using the afternoons to meander at leisure. La Maison Bleue is recommended for
a special dinner, but you must book (tel: 055-741843).*

Before entering Fez el Bali by Bab Boujeloud visit the excellent
Musée du Batha (8.30am–noon and 2.30– 6pm; closed Tues; admission charge), occupying a late 19th-century palace off Place l'Istiqlal.
It is en route and helps flesh out the mysteries of life within Fez el
Bali's walls. To get to the museum, take a taxi to Place l'Istiqlal
(alternatively, take a bus to Istiqlal, from Place de la Resistance in
the Nouvelle Ville) and walk up the street to the right of Hotel Batha
as you face it. The museum is 50 metres/yds up on the right.

Right: melon man

A Madrassa with a Tale to Tell

According to local sources – almost certainly unreliable in view of the Moroccans' love of cautionary tales – the origins of the Bou Inania Madrassa are rooted in a scandal. The Sultan Bou Inan was renowned for his high living and extensive harem (begetting 325 sons in 10 years), but there came a point in his dissolute life when, after falling deeply in love with a beautiful woman, he vowed to reform. He made the woman his wife and as a public display of his new-found piety he commissioned the Bou Inania Madrassa to be built on the site of public latrines inside Bab Boujeloud.

But unfortunately the object of his love was a former prostitute-dancer and his viziers, though impressed by the wondrous new *madrassa*, were outraged at its association with a whore. To justify his action, the clever sultan took them to the newly completed building. 'Did you not used to piss where now you pray?' he asked, inviting the dumbstruck dignitaries to see the parallel. From that moment the sultan's new wife was considered a pillar of respectability.

Inside, a series of *salles* open off a central garden. If your understanding of French is reasonable it's worth following the guide. At the moment the museum space is being used to house temporary, themed exhibitions. However, the museum is expected to revert to its usual format, described here, within the next couple of years. Each room is usually dedicated to one aspect of traditional Moroccan crafts and illustrates its application in everyday life over the centuries. Interesting oddities include a measuring vessel for determining the level of alms a wealthy Muslim should give *(salle 3)* and the collection of 14th-century doors (the small inner door was for people to pass through; the larger, outer one for beasts). Among the agricultural tools on display, note the necklace of bristles worn by male calves so that their mothers, prickled when their young came to suck, would kick them away, forcing them to graze on the herbs which made their meat particularly sweet.

From the museum, return down the street to Place l'Istiqlal and make a left turn past the Bibliotheca Batha. Follow the road round, keeping the walls

of the museum and library on your left. After a few minutes' walk the road emerges in front of the lovely **Bab Boujeloud**, a trio of keyhole arches embellished with blue *faïence*. Though of comparatively recent date (1919), Bab Boujeloud marks the threshold of **Fez el Bali**. Before passing under its arches, pause over a mint tea in one of the clutch of cafés hereabouts, or perhaps on the roof terrace of the Café du Kasbah just inside the gate.

Just inside Bab Boujeloud it is vital to make a left turn followed by a right to reach **Talaa Kebira**, the main vein of the medina. Talaa Kebira begins with a small but vividly Moroccan food market – bloody sheep's heads behind ragged curtains of tripe, mounds of mint, death rows of startled chickens. Beyond is a quieter stretch of diverse trades, with a *babouches* (slippers) seller here, a tap mender there, a nut roaster next door – trades and products which gradually separate into their own souks. To the left and right of the Talaa, archways lead to crumbling courtyards and *fondouks* (the old lodging houses of merchants), which are worth dipping into. A short way down the street a pair of brown doors on the left-hand side lead into a small grain market catering to those who still grind their own cereals.

The Bou Inania Madrassa

The Bou Inania Madrassa lies about 150 metres/yds along the Talaa Kebira, signalled by the heavy overhead scaffolding of restorers working on the

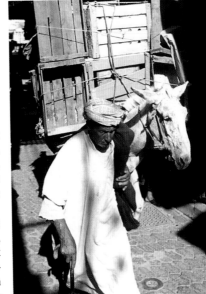

Bou Inania water-clock which would otherwise be clearly visible directly opposite the *madrassa*. This 14th-century clock, constructed at the behest of Sultan Bou Inan to ring out the hours of prayer, has been silent for five centuries. According to local myth the clock fell silent when a pregnant Jewess, alarmed by its chimes, miscarried her child. The discovery, in 1990, of an early 13th-century document describing the working of the clock led to reports of its imminent reawakening. But such optimism was premature: more than a decade has elapsed and the clock is still shrouded in scaffolding.

The **Bou Inania Madrassa** (9am–6pm; Fri 9–11am and 3–6pm; admission charge), on the right, is one of the most potent images of Morocco. It is one of the country's few buildings in religious use that can be entered by non-Muslims, though the invitation does not extend to the prayer hall. *Madrassas* were not normally used for public prayer, but Sultan Bou Inan wanted his *madrassa* to rival the Kairouyine Mosque; he even hoped that the call to prayer would be transferred here. No expense was spared on the interior decoration: the harmony of intricately carved cedar, lacy stucco, dazzling *zellige* and bands of Koranic verses is intended to represent the oneness of God. When the cost of this work

Left: Bab Boujeloud
Right: the streets of Fez el Bali are too narrow for cars

was added up Bou Inan is reputed to have tossed the accounts into the river. The *madrassa* is undergoing restoration, so some areas may be out of bounds, but, if possible, take a look at the students' quarters on the first floor.

Regaining the street, proceed along Talaa Kebira and through an arch, at which point the street begins to go downhill. After a short distance it passes, on the right, the one-time house (no admittance) of the14th-century Tunisian Ibn Khaldoun, who was famous for a seminal history of the Arabs.

Another five minutes' walk along the Talaa, opposite the stumpy white minaret of a mosque, an archway on the left leads to the butter and honey market, selling the expensive aged butter known as *smen*, culprit of the slightly rancid odour – at least to many Western noses – of the best *couscous*. Beyond this, the Talaa Kebira begins to narrow. Where it takes cover under a shady roof of rushes watch out for another turning on the left-hand side, this time leading to a courtyard where men sit paring the fat and remaining tissue from newly flayed hides.

After this the Talaa bends to the right. Beyond a small line of carpentry shops and bellows-makers it passes under a stone arch, to emerge in view of the tiled minaret of the late 18th-century **Cherrabliyne Mosque** (slipper-makers' Mosque), framed by the bulging upper storeys of buildings. Winding and descending still further, the street (now called Rue Cherrabliyne)

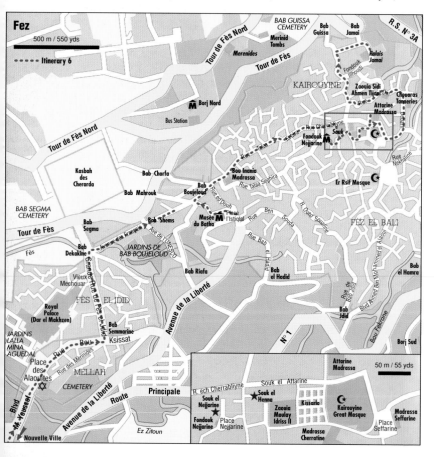

passes through another stone arch and enters a shopping area of grocers and hardware stalls. As the street levels out a sudden glut of leather and carpet bazaars signals the wealth of souks surrounding the Kairouyine Mosque.

The Souks

At a faded sign saying Souk el Henna, you need to take a sharp right. But before this, dip into Souk el Attarine (straight ahead on the main route), the perfume and spice souk, where if you are in need of lunch you can adjourn to Restaurant Saada, one of the better restaurants of its kind in the area. Like all the fully-fledged restaurants hereabouts it is a converted *dar* (house – see *Eating Out, page 75*), so you are likely to find it either empty, when the dining room seems gloomy, or packed with tour groups (they are always happy to squeeze in extras). If you can hold out without a lavish spread, eat on the hoof courtesy of street vendors – slices of tortilla, *sfenj* (doughnuts), *khobz bishemar* (a kind of samosa) and cactus fruits – or save yourself for a buffet lunch or tea in Palais Jamai.

Regaining the spot where you entered Souk el Attarine (with the entrance in front of you), strike right. The first turn on the left is the entrance to the aromatic and shady **Souk el Henna** (also accessible from Attarine), where baskets of green henna leaves, camomile, antimony (from which khol – eyeliner – is derived), pumice, red salves for the lips and cheeks and a tar-like black soap are some of the more orthodox items on offer. Love potions, including the urogenital stimulant Spanish Fly (beware: it can be dangerous), are a speciality.

Returning to where you entered Souk el Henna, turn left (away from Souk el Attarine) and take the second turning on the right to **Place Nejjarine** (carpenters) and the beautifully restored 17th-century **Nejjarine Fountain**, with its elaborately-tiled surround (Fez's fountains are potable), and the Fondouk Nejjarine *(see below)*. Off the *place* is the carpenters' souk, heavy with the scent of worked cedar and thuja wood. The small, painted octagonal trays are used in circumcision ceremonies for carrying the *m'tahar* (circumcised); the larger ones are used at weddings for carrying the bride and groom. For an illuminating insight into woodworking traditions in Morocco visit the finely restored 18th-century **Fondouk Nejjarine**, which has been turned into a **museum** (10am–5pm; admission charge) devoted to carpentry techniques and tools. Exhibits are well displayed and supported by interesting explanatory notes. The museum's attractive roof-top café (beverages only) offers views over the green roofs of the nearby Zaouia of Moulay Idriss II.

Above: the Nejjarine Fountain

The Zaouia of Moulay Idriss II

Return to the street from which you turned left into Place Nejjarine and, turning right, continue for a few metres before bearing left through a corridor of stalls selling incense and candles, the usual sign in Morocco that one is approaching a *zaouia* or tomb. In this case it's the **Zaouia of Moulay Idriss II**, who founded Fez in 809 (though some sources attribute this to his father, Idriss I). Proceed under a wooden bar (designed to block the passage of beasts and, at one time, infidels) to approach the *zaouia*. Entrance to the shrine itself is forbidden to non-Muslims, but you can peep into the ornate anteroom. Note the collection of chandeliers and clocks on the wall – fashionable offerings to the great Idriss in the 19th century.

Turn right as you face the shrine and take the first left, following the walls of the *zaouia* round (bearing in mind that shops cleave to the walls of the shrine); notice a brass slot for alms in the wall. At the end of this side of the *zaouia* go through a doorway, where you will be confronted by a shop selling fezzes. Turn immediately left into the **Kissaria**, a covered market selling the luxury goods traditionally sold in the vicinity of a Great Mosque, such as fine kaftans, expensive cloth, silk thread and *babouches*. The original Kissaria was burned down in 1954 and the current building is modern. After walking straight ahead, through the main aisle of kaftan booths, turn right into the far aisle of *babouches* outlets. This exits on the continuation of Rue Attarine, between the Attarine Madrassa (on the left) and the principal entrance to the Great Mosque of Kairouyine (on the right-hand side of the street straight ahead).

The **Attarine Madrassa** (8.30am–6pm; closed Fri am; admission charge), one of several *madrassas* situated around the Great Mosque of Kairouyine, was built by Sultan Abou Said from 1322–25 and is similar in design to the later Bou Inania at the start of this tour, albeit with a tiled rather than paved courtyard; no doubt many of the same master craftsmen worked on its interior. As the *madrassa* is no longer in religious use, you can enter the prayer hall, where the *mirhab* (embellished niche) orientates prayer towards Mecca. Good views over the blue and white tiled courtyard of the Kairouyine Mosque are to be had from the *madrassa's* roof (tip to gain access) if open (it was closed for renovation at the time of going to press).

One of the World's Oldest Universities

The **University Mosque of Kairouyine** – the largest mosque in Africa until the Hassan II Mosque was built in Casablanca – is the centre of Fez el Bali, to which all routes are said eventually to lead. The original mosque was built by Fatima el Feheri, a wealthy refugee from Kairouan, Tunisia, in memory

Above: a peek inside the Zaouia of Moulay Idriss II

of her home city, but it was considerably enlarged and altered later. Its simple minaret is 10th-century and the courtyard is 16th-century. It is closed to non-Muslims, but the entrances offer glimpses into its calm and airy courtyard.

Shops cling to the sides of the Great Mosque, so it is difficult always to discern its perimeter walls. However, keeping these on your right (every so often you will pass one of the mosque's 14 doors), walk clockwise round the mosque and eventually you reach, on a downward-sloping space in front of the Kairouyine library, **Place Seffarine**, the picturesque brassworkers' souk, heralded by the sound of hammering.

The Tanneries

From here, it is a straightforward walk to the tanneries on the Oued Fes. Take the exit next (clockwise) to the one from which you entered Place Seffarine.

After a few minutes' walk, taking the left route when you reach a T-junction, you come to **Chouaras Tanneries**, one of three in Fez, visible through a gap on the right-hand side of the street. Your nose will inform you of your arrival. This time the smell is pretty unpleasant – of fresh animal hides steeped in urine to make them supple. Sprigs of mint are proffered as pomanders. To get the best views of the eggbox network of pits where the skins are soaked and dyed, clamber up to the terraces, where the skins are laid to dry.

As rest and scented gardens are probably now in order, I recommend

Above: overview of Fez el-Bali
Left: kaftans in the Kissaria

a short hike up to the **Palais Jamai** for tea on the terrace by the swimming-pool. It isn't that far, but the route is a little tortuous. 'Toute droite,' the locals will say, and this is more or less true. First, turn right as you leave the tanneries and proceed until the route forks, at which point go left. Continue until you reach, on the left-hand side, the elaborate keyhole entrance of the **Zaouia of Sidi Ahmed Tijani**, a leading Sufi, and turn immediately right, passing under the wooden beam. Overhead you will see a sign (in the form of a star) indicating the route to Bab Guissa. Follow the clear indications all the way to Bab Guissa, passing along the way Cinema Hilal on your right and then climbing steeply for five minutes or so before arriving at an arch. Pass through the arch and turn right across the car park. From here the Palais Jamai is clearly visible.

Palais Jamai and the Merenid Tombs

This lovely hotel was built at the end of the 19th century as a palace by the Jamai brothers, viziers of Sultan Moulay Hassan. The brothers eventually fell foul of the political machinations of the day (including their own) and

when Moulay Abdelaziz succeeded to the throne in 1894 they were sent in fetters to Tetouan. Walter Harris, the correspondent of *The Times*, related their fate in his book *Morocco That Was*: 'In the course of time – and how long those ten years must have been – Haj Amaati died. The Governor of Tetouan was afraid to bury the body, lest he should be accused of having allowed his prisoner to escape. He wrote to Court for instructions. It was summer, and even the dungeon was hot. The answer did not come for eleven days, and all that time Si Mohammed Soreir remained chained to his brother's corpse.'

After reflecting on how the mighty fall, if you have regained some energy, walk up to the

Above: working in the tanneries
Left: one mint tea coming up

Merenid tombs on the hillside behind the hotel for extensive views. Otherwise take a taxi to your hotel.

Fez el Jdid

The best time to explore Fez el Jdid is two hours before sunset. Then the 13th-century Merenid city built alongside Fez el Bali (originally as a separate city with its own walls) is at its most animated – full of shopping Fassis – and pleasantly cool. Start from the long palm-lined Boulevard Moulay Youssef, in the Nouvelle Ville, and drift north with the crowd towards **Place des Alaouites**, across which the seven brass doors of the Royal Palace keep a haughty distance. With the walls of the Palace on your left, follow Rue Bou Ksissat past the *mellah* (former Jewish quarter), lined by shops selling dried fruits and pulses. The *mellah* was usually built close to the Royal Palace in medinas, so that the Jewish community received a degree of Royal protection. The word *mellah*, Arabic for salt, alludes to the Jews' job of salting the severed heads of the sultan's victims so that they would better sustain weathering when mounted on the city's gates, a practice current in Morocco until the early 20th century. One in a particularly impressive array of heads fell as a British minister, Sir Reginald Lister, passed beneath Bab Mharouk in 1909.

At Bab Semmarine (the first gate on your left), which separated the *mellah* and Muslim quarter, turn into Grande Rue de Fez el Jdid, a heaving souk devoted to domestic goods and cheap clothing. The noise and pace are invigorating. At the end of the souk proceed through an arch, which leads into the Petit Mechouar, enclosed by high, crenellated walls and bordered by the tradesmen's entrance to the Palace. The gate in front of you is Bab Dekakine, from which, in the mid-15th century, the dead brother of Henry the Navigator swung by his feet for four days, after his family refused to trade him for Ceuta, which the Portuguese had captured.

Instead of heading through Bab Dekakine, turn right into the quieter Avenue des Français, a shadowy shelter of romantic trysts, which runs alongside the Bab Boujeloud gardens. Before Bab Boujeloud the avenue dissolves into a car park and drop-off area for taxis. Hail one of the many *petit-taxis* to take you up to **Hotel Merenides**, perched near Borj Nord. This modern hotel was rebuilt after being razed to the ground in riots in 1990. Make your way to the terrace where, beverage in hand, you can watch the sun go down and the minarets light up. Afterwards I suggest you hail a taxi to take you to your choice of restaurant for dinner. **La Maison Bleue** (2 Place l'Istiqal; tel: 055-741843) is strongly recommended (be sure to book). Alternatively if you fancy good, inexpensive Italian/international cuisine, head for **Chez Vittorio's** in Rue Brahim Roudani in the new town.

Right: olives galore at a stand in Fez el Jdid

7. MOULAY IDRISS, VOLUBILIS AND MEKNES
(see maps, p46 and 48)

A day excursion from Fez, taking in Moulay Idriss, a town built around the shrine of Morocco's first sultan, the Roman ruins of Volubilis, and the city of Meknes, the imperial capital of Sultan Moulay Ismail.

This circular tour (about 130km/80 miles altogether) takes in major sites and pretty scenery. To do everything in one day, a car is recommended, but those without their own transport can do the journey in stages, beginning with a bus (one a day from the bus station under Borj Nord) or a grand-taxi (from Bab Boujeloud) to Moulay Idriss.

Making an early start, leave Fez for Moulay Idriss in a westerly direction on the N6 Meknes/Rabat road. After some 8km (5 miles), branch right towards Sidi Kacem/Ouezzane. At the small village of Nzala-des-Beni-Ammar take

a sharp left to Moulay Idriss and Volubilis (signposted). From here, a single-track road winds steeply through a hillocky landscape of olive groves, delivering you at **Moulay Idriss** after about 10km (6 miles).

After parking your car in the car park on the right as you enter town, walk down the hill to a central square with new arcades of shops and foaming fountains.

Moulay Idriss, a descendant of the Prophet via the line of Ali, and therefore a contender for the caliphate, was the founder of the first orthodox Muslim dynasty in Morocco (AD 788–91). Forced to flee from Baghdad after rebelling against the caliph Harun er Rashid (the hero of *The Thousand and One Nights*), he fled west and eventually found a home in Walili, formerly the Roman town of Volubilis. As a descendant of the Prophet, he was welcomed by the superficially Islamised Berber tribes and was proclaimed their leader. Idriss's son by his Berber concubine Kenza became Idriss II, the founder of Fez.

The town of Moulay Idriss evolved around the site of Idriss I's tomb on Mount Zerhoun near Volubilis. It is considered the holiest city in Morocco and hosts an important *moussem* at harvest time.

Non-Muslims were forbidden to enter Moulay Idriss until 1912 and the shrine itself is still out of bounds, but you may peer into its tiled courtyard from the entrance, reached through a string of stalls selling nougat and candles at the top of the square. A wooden bar is designed to repel beasts of burden and infidels from penetrating further into the sanctuary.

For an overview of the town, take the archway on the left as you face the shrine, and climb up the hill. Turn right at the drinking fountain, then left

Above: stalls selling candles usually flank important tombs or *zaouias*

through an arch and up some steps. Meander up until you reach a terrace which has good views of the green-tiled roofs of the shrine and town behind. To the right, in the middle distance, are the ruins of Volubilis, where Idriss I took refuge.

Returning to your car, pick up provisions for a picnic – bread, cheese, olives, fruit and a little of the ubiquitous nougat – from one of the *bachals* (grocer's) on the main street. To reach Volubilis, drive through the town centre and down the hill and then take the right fork. At the next junction take the road to Ouezzane (if you are travelling by public transport you will have to take a taxi or try to get a lift). Entrance to the site is on the left after 3km (2 miles).

Roman Outpost

Volubilis (8am–sunset; admission charge) is rarely busy, and sometimes you can have this idyllic spot to yourself. Though plundered by Moulay Ismail *(see page 47)* and damaged by an earthquake in 1755, the remains are extensive, with several mosaics still in situ. A programme of restoration was embarked upon in 1915, assisted by sketches made by an Englishman a few decades prior to the quake.

Volubilis was the capital of the Berber kingdom of Mauritania Tingitania under Juba II, a Roman-educated African married to the daughter of Mark Antony and Cleopatra. After annexation, from AD45–285, the city was the western outpost of Rome's North African provinces. It was a wealthy city, with a flourishing olive oil industry (used for fuel rather than cooking). Ancient olive presses are scattered all over the site, many in private villas.

The layout of the town is easy to grasp. After crossing the little bridge over the stream, follow the arrow along the left-hand footpath. Climbing up to the main part of the site, turn right and then left to join the main street (follow the arrow). The first point of interest is the **House of Orpheus**, marked by a clump of cypress trees down to the left of the cobbled street. Of its several mosaics, the most impressive is the one in the *triclinium* (dining room) depicting the myth of Orpheus enchanting an assortment of wild animals. A black and white mosaic in the central atrium illustrates Amphitrite in a chariot being pulled by a sea-horse.

From the House of Orpheus, cut up to the square building containing a reconstructed olive press. Next to it are the **Thermes de Gallienus**, the most lavish public baths in the city, as their proximity to Volubilis's main civic buildings – the Capitol, Basilica and Forum – required.

Right: mosaic in the House of Orpheus, Volubilis

The raised building to the right of the main path, distinguished by a crop of free-standing Corinthian pillars and a flight of 13 steps on its north side, is the **Capitol** (temple), dedicated to Jupiter, Juno and Minerva, the deities associated with protection of the state. Adjoining it is the **Basilica** (law courts/administrative building), divided into five aisles by the stumpy remnants of columns.

Before you reach the distinctive Triumphal Arch, look out to the left for the **House of the Acrobat** (signposted Maison aux Desauteur). The **Triumphal Arch**, erected in AD217 by Marcus Aurelius Sebastenus in honour of the Emperor Caracella, marks the beginning of the Decumanus Maximus, the broad street running up to the **Tangier Gate**. Before walking to the top, investigate the **House of Ephebus**, with vivid mosaics in the rooms off its central courtyard, and the **House of Columns**.

Impressive villas flank the grandiose Decumanus Maximus. It is worth poking about; the villas are set back from the street, which originally would have been lined by small shops. Further up,

Volubilis

200 m / 220 yds

Tangier Gate

North Gate

Gordien Palace

House of the Four Seasons

House of the Labours of Hercules

House of the Nereids

House of Venus

House of Columns

Knight's House

House of Ephebus

Triumphal Arch

Fountain

Maison aux Desauteur (House of the Acrobat)

Forum

Basilica

Capitol

Temple of Saturn

Fertassa

Thermes de (Baths of) Gallienus

Twin Temples

House of Orpheus

Parking

Entrance

Meknes

Open-air Museum

Above: the Triumphal Arch, Volubilis. **Right:** Bab Mansour

is the **Knight's House**, with its mosaic of Dionysus discovering Ariadne asleep; the **House of the Labours of Hercules**, with a mosaic depicting the said labours; the **House of the Four Seasons**; and eventually the **Gordien Palace**, seat of the governor. After the Gordian Palace, turn right and return towards the Basilica and Capitol via a clearly defined street running parallel with Decumanus Maximus. This way, you pass on the left the **House of Venus**, marked by a single cypress tree, with its mosaics of Diana surprised by Acteon while bathing with her nymphs, and on the right the **House of the Nereids**.

Following the footpath and keeping the small hill in the middle of the site on your right, meander round towards the river near the entrance. Trees provide shade for your well-earned picnic. Aim to depart from Volubilis by 2pm in order to leave a full afternoon in Meknes.

Meknes

For **Meknes**, proceed back towards Moulay Idriss, but carry on along the main road instead of turning up to the town (if you are travelling by public transport, take a *grand-taxi* or bus from Moulay Idriss). After 24km/15 miles the road brings you into Rue Congo Al Moutahida in Meknes's new town. At the roundabout, turn down Avenue Moulay Ismail and cross the river to the old city lying on the west bank. Follow the one-way system round to Bab Mansour (signposted). Park in the large car park on the right of the road, beyond and below the gate.

Bab Mansour, a massive triple-bayed gate incorporating two marble columns plundered from Volubilis, is the centrepiece of Meknes. On one side is Place el Hedim (Place of Death), now a fine square with fountains, leading into the medina, and on the other, through its portals, is Place Lalla Aouda (to the left) and the entrance to Moulay Ismail's imperial city.

A member of the Alaouite dynasty (and therefore a forerunner of Morocco's current king), Moulay Ismail became sultan of Morocco in 1672 and ruled for 55 years. Unlike previous sultans who had ruled from Fez, Marrakesh or Rabat, he broke with tradition and ruled from Meknes (where he had previously been pasha), a city that offered unlimited scope for his megalomaniacal building schemes. He emulated Louis XIV and planned a palace on the scale of Versailles. At one point he hoped that one of the Sun King's daughters might join his 500-strong harem.

The remains of Moulay Ismail's imperial city, contained by some 25km (15 miles) of massive walls built by 2,000 Christian slaves and 30,000 other prisoners (some reputedly immured in the fruit of their own labour), are the highlights of Meknes. But before exploring these, visit the **Madrassa Bou Inania** (daily 9am–noon and 2–4pm; admission charge) in the medina. The most direct way to reach it is through Bab Aissa, an inconspicuous gate (signposted) some 50 metres/yds from Place el Hedim. This leads straight to the *madrassa's* magnificent bronze door.

Though begun by the Merenid sultan Abou el Hassan, the building was completed by, and thus named after his son, Abou Inan, in the mid-14th century. It is similar to the other Merenid *madrassas*, with a central fountain in a tiled courtyard, student quarters on two levels and a prayer hall on one side. As usual, every centimetre of the central courtyard is painstakingly covered in abstract designs to mesmerising effect, a device designed to focus the mind on God.

The Imperial City

Retrace your steps to Bab Mansour, and walk through its main gate. Proceed straight ahead, passing **Place Lalla Aouda**, a shady square where women come to take the air in the late afternoon. The road then sweeps round to the right. Shortly afterwards, behind some railings on the right, is the **Koubbet el Khiyatin** and the so-called **prison of the Christians** (daily 9am–noon and 3–6.30pm; admission charge), a complex of subterranean vaults that once stretched 7km (4 miles) each way. According to the guide, the French blocked off most of the complex after a French couple and their dog went down to explore and never returned. There are two theories regarding the purpose of the complex: either that it was an enormous granary or that it housed 60,000 Christian prisoners who were victims of Barbary Coast piracy, in which Moulay Ismail had a controlling interest. The incisions visible in the pillars may have harnessed their shackles. No light penetrated this Stygian place – the holes in the roof were made by the French.

Leaving here, walk through the double gate decorated with blue tiles. On the left is the **tomb of Moulay Ismail** (also open to non-Muslims 8am–1pm and 3–7pm, closed Fri). Moulay Ismail is venerated as a great sultan to this day, not least because he was the first ruler to subdue the *bled es siba*, the area beyond the more manageable towns of the coast and plains. The tomb was restored by his descendant, the late Mohammed

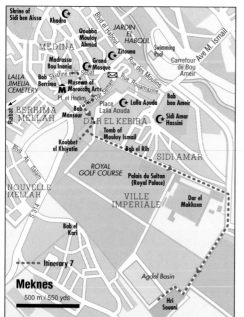

Meknes

500 m / 550 yds

Top Right: Heri Souani
Right: Place el Hedim

V. The clocks you see were given to Ismail by Louis XIV in 1700, in lieu of his daughter.

Leaving the tomb, turn left through the double layer of city walls, following the sign for Heri Souani (Dar el Ma). (This is a long but easy walk with shade provided by the pockmarked walls; if you are tired or hot, flag down a *petit-taxi*.) After bearing right, the route passes through a tunnel and emerges in the *mechouar,* with the Royal Palace on the right. Keep straight, passing through a set of double arches, and continue to the **Heri Souani** (Dar el Ma; daily 7am–12.30pm and 3–6pm; admission charge), where Moulay Ismail stored grain to feed his army), with the **Agdal basin**, a reservoir built by Moulay Ismail in case of siege, to the right. Before entering the granaries, you can recover from your hike and survey the surrounding ruins from the garden of the café perched on its roof (up the steps to the right of the entrance). Refreshed, take a quick peek inside the granaries before they close.

Back to Fez

Afterwards, take a taxi back to Bab Mansour. Relax on a bench on Place el Hedim or dip into the **souks** (reached through the gate on the left on the far side of Place el Hedim), which should be warming up for an early evening surge of shoppers. Leave Meknes via the new town for Fez (*grand-taxis* from the car-park at Place el Hadim).

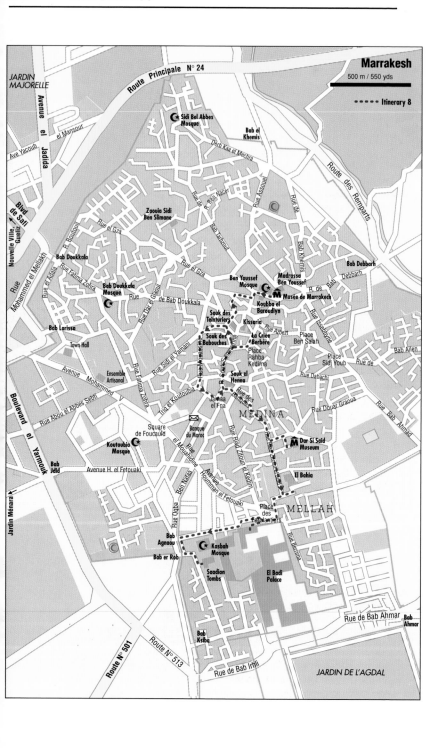

Marrakesh

Set on a wide, pinkish plain below the Atlas Mountains, Marrakesh is the capital of southern Morocco. Founded by Youssef ben Tashfine of the Almoravides, a conquering Berber dynasty that blew up like a desert storm in the 11th century, it evolved as a rendezvous for the great trade caravans plying the trans-Saharan salt, gold, sugar and slave routes between Fez and domains to the south. It tended to alternate with Fez as the country's capital; the Almohads and the Saadians both ruled from here, the former building the Koutoubia Mosque, the lovely minaret of which is the main orientation point in the city.

Marrakesh still has an African rather than an Arab beat, and it has a semi-desert climate, as the *pisé* (mud and palm fibre) buildings suggest. Though it is watered by the melted snows of the Atlas and is surprisingly verdant, in summer, from June through September, temperatures can soar over 37°C (98°F), making escapes to the mountains or the coast desirable after spending a couple of days in the city.

The City's Layout

Gueliz, the *nouvelle ville*, named after a range of small hills, is set apart from the medina by the long Avenue Mohammed V. Though not as exotic as the medina, it is attractive, with lush gardens, a lively café and restaurant scene, and the majority of the city's hotels. On the northeastern edge of the city, sandwiched between the Casablanca and Fez roads is the *palmeraie*, said to have sprung up from the discarded date stones of the Almoravide army. A desirable residential area, the *palmeraie* is dotted with palatial villas.

The medina radiates from the Jamaa el Fna, a large, irregular-shaped market cum circus, whose nightly entertainments have transfixed visitors for centuries. The Jamaa el Fna is often translated as 'Place of the Dead', but those attuned to the subtleties of Arabic translate it as 'Place of the Apocalypse', a more fitting description of the hellraising intensity of the Jamaa at about 9pm on a stifling summer evening, when the assorted cries and sweating faces of hawkers, conjurers, fortune-tellers, fakirs and tooth-pullers loom and fade through the smoke from scores of braziers. Evening on the Jamaa should on no account be missed, but hold on to your wallets – professional pickpockets operate on the square.

Right: a water-seller poses

8. THE MARRAKESH EXPERIENCE *(see map, p50)*

Orientation over breakfast overlooking the Jamaa el Fna. Then a tour of the souks and the sights of the northern medina, including the Madrassa Ben Youssef and the dyers' quarter. After lunch, a tour of the southern medina, including the Bahia and Badi palaces and the Saadian Tombs.

This full day-tour of the city divides into morning and afternoon itineraries, both starting from the Jamaa el Fna. If you are in Marrakesh in summer, when heat kills the desire for much sightseeing, spread the tour over two mornings, using your afternoons to cool down in a hotel pool or take a calèche to the Menara gardens or the Jardin Majorelle, off the Fez road. The souks should be avoided in early to mid afternoon, when they are mainly closed.

If you want to splash out and dine like a pasha at least once on your visit to Morocco, Marrakesh – a sybarite's city – is a good place to indulge. You need to book your restaurant (or get your hotel to do it for you) before setting off for the day. Yacout, Tobsil (both very expensive) and La Palais Gharnatta are all recommended *(see Eating Out, page 79).*

Before beginning a tour of the north of the medina, where the souks and Madrassa ben Youssef are, take stock of its layout over breakfast on the roof terrace of the Café de France overlooking the southern leg of the Jamaa el Fna. Also from here is a good view of the minaret of the 12th-century **Koutoubia Mosque**, one of a trio of distinctively similar minarets that epitomised the flowering of Almohad culture in North Africa and Spain (the others being the Giralda in Seville and the Tour Hassan in Rabat). The mosque marks the point where the medina ends and the long hike to Gueliz starts. Alongside the tower, the ruins of the rest of the original Almoravide mosque have been excavated, and the pleasant piazza and garden are a gathering point for families and friends in the early evening.

The Souks

The entrance to the northern part of the medina lies directly opposite the Café de France. It leads straight into **Souk el Henna** (signposted), though henna leaves are almost invisible among the banks of nuts, dates and dried figs.

At the end of the souk, go through a large keyhole gate of lacy stucco into Rue Semmarine. The souks of Marrakesh, not as well defined as those of Fez, can seem like a treacherous maze. As Elias Canetti, in *Voices of Marrakesh*, observed: 'You find everything – but you find it many times over.' To cut out this bewildering sense of disorientation, simplify your route by dipping into the many alleyways and courtyards leading off Rue Semmarine but always return to this main drag.

Rue Semmarine is varied in its merchandise. Shops selling *babouches*, kaftans and cloth are interspersed with upmarket tourist bazaars. After some 10 minutes of ambling, a turning on the right leads to **Rahba Kedima**, an irregular-shaped *place* which in turn leads to a wool market, a clutch of apothecary stalls and, off to the left at the far end of the area, the Criée Berbère, which until 1915 was used for auctioning slaves.

Retrace your steps to Rahba Kedima and thence to Rue Semmarine. Where this forks, shortly afterwards, take the left route, which feeds into Souk des Babouches and then Souk des Tailleurs, devoted to haberdashery. At the next fork, take the right lane. Soon afterwards, turn left into a narrow avenue of ironmongers, and proceed to the end. From this point the green-tiled minaret of the Ben Youssef Mosque is clearly visible about 100 metres/yds away. Zigzag towards it through a busy leathermakers' souk and at the end turn into Place Kissaria Ben Youssef, a dusty open space bordered by walls.

Almoravide Remains

The **Ben Youssef Mosque** is directly in front of you. Though this particular model dates from the 19th century, a mosque has existed here since the

11th century. The Almoravide sultan Youssef ben Tashfin is supposed to have laboured on the original building with his own hands. Non-Muslims are not permitted to enter the mosque, but they may visit the **Koubba el Baroudiyn** (9am–6.30pm), an annexe once used for ablutions, which is the only surviving Almoravide structure in Marrakesh. Its entrance is opposite the mosque, along the wall to the right. The *koubba* was unearthed from rubble in 1947. There isn't much to see, just a simply decorated two-storey

Left: night falls on the Jamaa el Fna
Above and Right: in the souks

structure with dome, but the *koubba* was of seminal importance in the development of Hispano-Mauresque architecture. The motifs and style you see here – the step battlements, the key-hole arches, the carving inside its dome – have been repeated and elaborated through eight centuries of North African art and architecture.

For the nearby **Madrassa Ben Youssef** (9am–6pm; closed Fri am; admission charge), turn right as you leave the *koubba* and then left, past the new Musée de Marrakech (*see below*); its metal door is on the right. The largest of the *madrassas* (living quarters for religious students) in Morocco, it was built by the Saadian sultan Abdullah el Ghalib in the 16th century to outdo the *madrassas* built in key cities all over Morocco by the Merenids. The sultan's burning ambition was for Marrakesh to eclipse the religious and intellectual standing of Fez; consequently the *madrassa* was finished within a year. Inside, look out for a marble basin decorated with eagles and vegetation; an inscription says that it was made for an Ommayed chamberlain, known to have lived in Spain in the 10th century. Animate decoration like this, taboo according to strict interpretations of the Koran, is rare in Morocco.

Next to the *madrassa* is the privately-owned **Musée de Marrakech** (9am–6.30pm; admission charge), occupying the sumptuously decorated 19th-century Palais Mnebhi, which belonged to a vizier of Sultan Moulay Abdelaziz (1894–1908). As well as displaying a fine collection of calligraphy from all over the Muslim world, the museum holds modern art exhibitions and has an excellent bookshop (great for lavish coffee-table books on Morocco) and a courtyard café. Don't miss the extensive *hammam*, containing 18th-and 19th-century watercolours and lithographs of Moroccan seaports.

Leaving the museum, retrace your steps through the leathermakers and ironmongers. Heading back towards Jamaa el Fna, take the first archway on your right, which leads into the **Souk des Teinturiers** (souk of the dyers), flagged by skeins of coloured wool set out to dry over the adjacent alleyways. Towards the end of the main street, you pass an elaborate drinking fountain built, like the *madrassa*, by Sultan Abdulla el Ghalib. Just past here, turn left into Rue Mouassine, following the walls of the Mouassine Mosque. This is the best route back to the Jamaa el Fna.

Above: carpets are hard to resist
Right: the Madrassa Ben Youssef

The Palaces

Leaving the delights of the Jemma until later (they are comparatively desultory in the heat of the day), make your way to the point outside the Café de France where this tour began. As you face the café, look to the left and you will see Chez Chergaouni, a basic restaurant with a terrace a couple of buildings in from Rue des Banques. The food is cheap and tasty and, if you sit on the terrace, you will find plenty of entertaining action on the street below. After taking a leisurely break (bearing in mind that the custodians of Morocco's museums and monuments tend do the same), strike into the southern quarter of the medina, for the Dar Si Said museum, the Bahia and Badi palaces and the Saadian Tombs, the remnant of Marrakesh's imperial past.

The starting point is Rue des Banques, the first street on the left as you turn left out of the restaurant, which bears right at Hotel Mounir into Rue Zitoun el Jdid (not signposted). After a 5-minute walk or so, there is a 'no-entry for vehicles' sign. Proceed through here and, if you want to visit the museum, take the first left past the police station, following the signpost to the museum, which is marked by a red flag.

The **Dar Si Said Museum** (9am–12.15pm and 3–6.45pm, closed Tues; admission charge) occupies a 19th-century palace that belonged to the brother of Bou Ahmed, Sultan Abdelaziz's chamberlain and grand vizier, who resided at the nearby El Bahia. The brothers were the sons of a negro slave, but thanks to Bou Ahmed's Machiavellian gifts (Si Said was, in the clinical sense of the word, an idiot), they had risen to positions of influence.

The museum housed a varied collection of exhibits, including children's toys and the usual examples of doors and *mashrabiya* (wooden screens), weaponry, jewellery and a large collection of copper, brass and silverware. Among the latter are kettles with a compartment for burning the charcoal, conical-lidded containers for holding bread, long-spouted vessels for pouring water over the hands of dinner guests, and incense holders – the latter two essential preludes and postscripts to any elaborate meal in a traditional

Above: the Dyers' souk

household to this day). The first floor has a marriage chair, used for carrying the bride to her new home, and there is an extensive collection of carpets.

Back on Rue Riad Zitoun el Jdid, it is only 100 metres/yds or so to the end of the street and, on the left, **El Bahia** (8.45–11.15am and 2.45–5.45pm, Fri 8.45–11.30am and 3–5.45pm; admission charge), Bou Ahmed's 19th-century palace. The practice of charging an official entrance fee has been abolished in favour of making the use of a guide obligatory (one with limited English is available). The palace is now officially part of the Royal Palace and parts of it are still used, mainly for guests.

Given the facts and figures reeled off by the guide, the palace is actually surprisingly unimpressive. El Bahia, which translates as 'the brilliant', named in honour of Bou Ahmed's first wife, was built at the public's expense over six years. Bou Ahmed, the chief vizier to Sultan Abdelaziz (the penultimate sultan prior to the French protectorate who did most to accelerate European encroachment), ousted the Jamai brothers – whose own palace in Fez is now the Palais Jamai Hotel – from rival positions of influence. Without him, Abdelaziz was a nonentity. Among the highlights are El Bahia's mosque, in particular the ceiling of the ablutions chamber, the harem for Bou Ahmed's 24 concubines and the separate premises of his four official wives. The chimneys and radiators were added during the French protectorate, when the palace functioned as the French Residency.

Leaving El Bahia, continue straight ahead. This area verges on the old *mellah* and you may notice junk/antiques shops hereabouts selling Jewish paraphernalia. Follow the road round, passing Douriya restaurant on your left and then cut left into a square. Cross this to pass through an arch. The entrance to El Badi Palace, signalled by a flag, is about 50 metres/yds to the right.

El Badi (8.30–11.45am and 2.30–5.45pm; admission charge), built in the late 16th century by the Saadian Ahmed el Mansur, is now a massive ruin

---

The Gardens of Marrakesh

The gardens of Marrakesh have always surprised and delighted visitors. The British writer Osbert Sitwell, in *Escape With Me*, called Marrakesh 'the ideal African city of water-lawns, cool, pillared palaces and orange groves.' In Islam, gardens are earthly intimations of paradise, the Eden of the afterlife described in the Koran as 'gardens watered by running streams'.

As well as the Jardin Majorelle, described in the itinerary above, Marrakesh has two other famous gardens, the Agdal and the Menara, which were originally agricultural estates where the sultan would grow olives and citrus fruits for profit. The smaller and more famous of the two, the Menara, about 2km (1 mile) along the Avenue de la Menara from Bab Jdid, is a pleasant ride away by *calèche*. If you want to see the snow-covered Atlas rising over its summer pavilion, a view captured on countless postcards, you need to time your visit for sunset in the first few months of the year.

crowned by storks' nests. It was ransacked at the end of the 17th century by Sultan Moulay Ismail, who wanted its prodigious marble for his own palace in Meknes. Apart from its sheer size, there is little to indicate the fabulous luxury reported by ambassadors who visited the palace in its heyday. Ahmed el Mansur, otherwise known as The Golden owing to his expeditions to gold-rich Timbuktu, employed artisans from all over the world to work on the palace, which was funded by profits from sugar production in the Souss Valley (sugar was exchanged for Italian marble pound for pound). All that remain today, however are the dry basins and their fountains and traces of the pavilions. Nonetheless it makes an atmospheric setting for an annual folklore festival in June.

The Saadian Tombs

The **Saadian Tombs** (daily 8.30–11.45am and 2.30–5.45pm; admission charge), the last site on this itinerary, are almost next door to El Badi, but it is necessary to circumvent El Badi's walls to reach the entrance. As you leave

El Badi, take the first archway on the left into a short street leading on to a small roundabout. Take the first left off the roundabout and proceed past the Ambra photographic studio. After a straight stretch the road bears left and immediately right (in a hindleg); proceed straight for some 200 metres/yds. Immediately before the end of the street, cut through an arch on the left. Pass through two further arches and then turn left, with the Bab Agnaou on your right towards the brown doors of the 12th-century Kasbah Mosque. As you turn right at the mosque you will see a sign indicating the narrow entrance to the Tombeaux Saadiens – specially cut to allow access to non-Muslims, prevented from entering via the Kasbah Mosque.

This small cemetery, admired for its refinement, was walled in by Moulay Ismail while he was destroying El Badi, and not rediscovered until 1917, when its existence was noted on aerial photographs taken by the French. It contains the slender tombstones of 66 members of the Saadian dynasty, plus favoured members of the royal household. The tomb of Ahmed el Mansur, the sultan who built El Badi, is in the centre of the three-chamber mausoleum on the left as you enter. Stalactite stucco, a trademark of the Saadian dynasty, is visible above the tombstone. The second mausoleum, at right-angles to the first, contains the tomb of Mohammed esch Sheik, the founder of the dynasty.

From here, walk back to **Bab Agnaou** (Almohad, and generally thought to be the most elegant gate in Marrakesh) where you can pick up a *petit-taxi* and head back to your hotel.

Left: El Badi Palace
Right: the beautifully decorated Saadian Tombs

If you have split this tour over two days and have some time to spare, take a *calèche* to the stunning **Jardin Majorelle**, off the Fez road (daily 8am–5.30pm; admission charge), a garden designed in the 1920s by the painter Jacques Majorelle, which has been beautifully restored by the former couturier Yves St Laurent.

Evening Options

A good way to launch an evening in Marrakesh is with a coffee outside the Brasserie du Glacier on the edge of the **Jamaa el Fna**. Here you can witness the action on the Jamaa heat up as the sun goes down. When the temperature feels about right, plunge into the crowds. The adrenalin-pumping sense of danger is not entirely misplaced: not so long ago one of the most experienced entertainers on the square died after being stung by his own scorpion.

After you have had your fill of snake charmers, storytellers and trance music, it may be time to think about dinner. If you have booked a restaurant hail a *calèche* to take you there. Alternatively, rub shoulders with the *Marrakshis* at one of the many stalls offering a host of tasty options, such as snails in liquor flavoured with cumin, sizzling *merguez* sausages, calves' feet with chickpeas and raisins and *harira* (the mutton soup of Ramadan). Afterwards tour the city's gates by *calèche*.

Either way, end the evening in the habit of Winston Churchill with a

nightcap in the *de trop* splendour of **La Mamounia Hotel** (Avenue Bab Jdid), a former palace and considered one of the great hotels of the world. The piano bar is open until the early hours, but if you want something more up tempo and are suitably dressed you can adjourn to the hotel's nightclub, or the casino.

Above: quiet corner in Jardin Majorelle
Left: take a *calèche*

9. EXCURSION TO ESSAOUIRA *(see map, p60–61)*

An excursion from Marrakesh to a fortified coastal town for sea air on the battlements, a lunch of grilled sardines and an afternoon on the beach.

To reach Essaouira, leave Marrakesh by Avenue Hassan II, which runs alongside the railway station. If you are travelling by public transport, catch a bus at Bab Doukkala, but check departure times in advance. If you want to stay in Essaouira, book a hotel room in advance from Marrakesh (see page 91 for choices).

Essaouira, formerly known as Mogador, lies on the Atlantic, 176km (110 miles) west of Marrakesh across a broad and stony plain. It is one in a series of fortified towns on the Atlantic coast. After the red walls and baking heat of Marrakesh, its blue and white medina and stiff sea breezes are refreshing (even in mid-summer temperatures do no more than nudge 24° or 25°C (the mid-70s °F), as is its laid-back character.

After a drive of two hours (three by bus) along the N8, the town appears low against an outcrop of rocks above a fine, sandy beach. Boulevard Mohammed V, the road into town, leads to a convenient car-park outside the harbour (buses other than CTM deposit passengers at the bus station at the back of town, from where it is best to take a taxi to the edge of Place Moulay Hassan). Leaving your car here, cross the wide pedestrianised **Place Moulay Hassan**, an afternoon assembly place for the well-concealed women of the town, to where it narrows into a café-lined avenue, a good place to relax over a coffee or cold drink and learn about the town's history.

Essaouira's History

In the 7th century the islands opposite the town were stop-offs for Phoenician sailors on their trading forays down the west coast of Africa. Later, they were developed as bases for the manufacture of a coveted dye derived from the murex shellfish. Known as Tyrian purple, the dye was used for the togas of Rome's elite. Under the Arabs, the mainland was developed as a trading port, leading to its occupation by the Portuguese in the 16th century.

The town that you see today was built entirely by Sultan Sidi Mohammed in the 1760s, to replace Agadir as Marrakesh's chief port. A French architect, a prisoner of the sultan, was employed on the project, hence the town's grid layout. To boost trade with Europe, the sultan removed all tariffs on imports and encouraged the settlement of Jews, who acted as intermediaries between the European merchants and local traders. The European and Jewish community grew – Benjamin Disraeli's father spent his early years in the *mellah* (Jewish quarter)

Right: battlemented Essaouira

of Mogador – and the economy flourished. Mogador became Morocco's main export point for oil and gum, and its leading shippers were known as 'hundred tonners' on account of the minimum weight they would ship at one time.

The Battlements

Place Moulay Hassan is where you are most likely to be approached by a would-be guide. In fact, the battlements with their line of bronze cannon (a location for Orson Welles's *Othello*) and the carpentry souk are the only real sights of the town and they are easy to find. To reach them, backtrack up Place Moulay Hassan towards the sea and cut right down Rue de Souka. After about 5 minutes you will reach an arch leading directly to the battlements, the round tower of the north bastion and the fragrant carpentry workshops housed in their undercarriage.

Return through the medina via Rue Laalou el Atterine instead of Rue de Souka. This way you pass a small **folklore museum** (9am–noon and 2.30–6pm; admission charge) and emerge on Avenue Oqba ibn Nafaa. By turning right here, you can return to Place Moulay Hassan and then turn into the harbour for an *al fresco* lunch of grilled sardines.

Afterwards sample the beach. If it is too breezy for swimming, take a bracing walk along the sands towards **Diabat** (7km/4 miles), a small village with a *plage sauvage* which Jimi Hendrix tried to buy in the late 1960s. This should work up an appetite for dinner at Chez Sam's or Chalet de la Plage *(see page 78)*, good reasons for travelling to Essaouira in themselves.

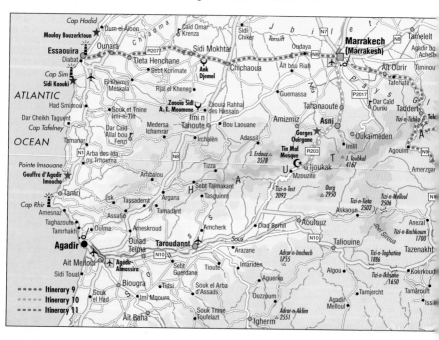

10. INTO THE ATLAS MOUNTAINS *(see map below)*

A two-day trip from Marrakesh. See the Tin Mal Mosque, seat of the Almohad dynasty, and go hiking in the Toubkal National Park.

Although a car is useful for this itinerary, it is possible to travel to Asni from Marrakesh by bus (from Bab Doukkala or Bab er Rob) or grand-taxi (from Bab er Rob). Before setting off, book a room in Asni's 3-star Grand Hotel du Toubkal (tel: 044-448872), which is due to reopen in 2002. You should also pack some warm clothing and walking boots. Leaving Marrakesh from Bab er Rob, take the R203 in the direction of Taroudannt.

In autumn and winter the snowcapped Atlas are clearly visible from Marrakesh and the beguiling prospect of snow in Africa never fails to attract visitors. But late spring and early summer, when the mountains vanish behind the haze encasing Marrakesh, is the best time to sample the Atlas.

The village of **Asni**, 46km (28 miles) from Marrakesh (market on Saturday), lies at the base of Toubkal, the highest mountain in North Africa (4,167metres/13,750ft), and makes a good springboard for exploring the region (there is also accommodation at Imlil and Ouirgane). To make the most of this trip, set off early, so that you arrive in Asni in time for breakfast in one of the Berber cafés in the village. Afterwards head up to Imlil (17km/10 miles), signposted to the left just beyond the village, to fix up the following day's trek. The road deteriorates after 12km (7 miles), but it can be tackled by a small car; alternatively buy a place in one of the trucks that ply the route.

Climbing Toubkal

Imlil, the highest of a string of picturesque hamlets along the valley, is watered by the Oued Moulay Brahim, which in spring and autumn tumbles over a fall

of boulders behind the village (at other times the river may be no more than a trickle). To organise the following day's hike, seek out the Bureau des Guides in the village, whose official guides *(accompagnateurs)* can organise all aspects of the climb. They may persuade you to take the two-day trek to Toubkal's summit, staying overnight in the mountain refuge. If it is late spring or summer and you have time, this can be an attractive option (the guide can supply specialist equipment such as crampons

Left: women of Essaouira

and icepicks if necessary). Otherwise just take the one-day trek up to the refuge, a combination of mule riding (lower slopes only) and hiking requiring only moderate fitness. Prices for mule hire, a mountain guide and food are set and published. If business is slack they may be negotiable. Any extras also cost, including the early morning pick-up which can be organised from your hotel (it is a 6am start).

The Valley of the Nfis

With your next day's itinerary organised, return down the valley to Asni, but instead of turning right into the village, turn left into the **Valley of the Nfis**, the one-time territory of the powerful Goundafi tribe. At the end of the 19th century Tayeb el Goundafi, one of the three principal Lords of the Atlas, could raise an army of 5,000 armed men. This is a beautiful afternoon ride, offering stunning vistas and, if there is plenty of water about,

opportunities to swim in the foaming Nfis River (no nude bathing, however deserted it looks). Drive up beyond Ijoukak to see the **Tin Mal Mosque** (signposted *site historique* and reached by a rickety bridge), where Ibn Toumert, the founder of the powerful Almohad dynasty that swept through North Africa and Spain in the 12th century, first rallied support.

On your return, stop for dinner (from 7pm) at **Au Sanglier qui Fume** in Ouirgane (on the right-hand side of the road), a former hunting lodge (licensed) where you can eat homely French food under the glassy glare of mounted trophies. For more refined dining, try **La Roseraie** nearby, an exclusive hotel run by a former manager of La Mamounia. Either way, remember your early morning start.

Above: Berber village
Left: the 12th-century Tin Mal Mosque

11. To Ouarzazate and the Draa Valley
(see map, p60–61)

A two-day excursion (there and back) from Marrakesh through the Atlas mountains via the Tizi-n-Tichka Pass to Ouarzazate, the gateway to the southern oases. Includes a detour to Telouet, ruined eyrie of the once powerful Glaoui family. A third day could be spent exploring the Draa Valley (highly recommended), staying overnight in Zagora.

Taxis and buses (from Bab Doukala) ply the Tizi-n-Tichka Pass between Marrakesh and Ouarzazate (grand-taxis complete the switchback ride of 190km (118 miles) in four hours, but to enjoy the scenery to the full your own transport is necessary. This route can be impassable in mid-winter (check with Tourist Office). For inexpensive, pleasant accommodation in Ouarzazate (reserve in advance), try the 2-star Hotel La Gazelle (pool, garden and restaurant, but no air-conditioning, tel: 044-882151), or the 3-star Hotel Riad Salam (tel: 044-883335). If you intend to spend another day exploring the Draa Valley, book a hotel in Zagora (Hotel La Fibule de Draa, tel: 044-847318, and Kasbah Asmaa, tel: 044-847241, are pleasant good-value options with pools, but there are several more upmarket choices available). Pack a picnic for the journey.

The N9 to the Tizi-n-Tichka pass leaves Marrakesh via Bab Rhemat (southeast side of the medina). After a 32 km (20-mile) drive across the plain, the road climbs into the Atlas foothills and a landscape filled with silver birch trees, palms and firs sprinkled with *pisé* (mud and palm fibre) villages. From here, each new twist in the road leads to ever more dramatic scenery. Fir plantations yield to the lush crops and olive groves of Toufliat, which in turn submit to sheer and barren mountainsides. After Tizela, the road joins a river and squeezes through a gorge, passing many pleasant spots in which to unpack your picnic and have a paddle if the riverbed isn't dry.

After Taddert, the road climbs steeply up to the col, the highest point on the pass. A kilometre or so before the summit, stop for mint tea or coffee (served with goat's or sheep's milk) at Café Tichka, spectacularly sited in the lap of Jebel Bou Ourioul.

The Mountain Stronghold of Telouet

Three kilometres (2 miles) after the café, take a sharp left (bumpy but surfaced) to **Telouet** (20km/12 miles), the ruined seat of the Glaoui clan, whose leaders, two ambitious brothers, Thami and Madani El Glaoui, were extremely influential during the French protectorate. Telouet rises in the middle of a remote valley, the few sparkling green tiles left on the kasbah's turrets hint-

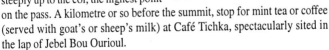

Right: the ruins of Telouet

ing at its former grandeur. It lies on the main pass through this part of the Atlas before the Tizi-n-Tichka was developed by the French in 1936. A vast warren of stone and *pisé* buildings, it is an accretion of countless generations of kasbahs.

Drive through the village, inhabited by the families of former employees and slaves of the Glaoui, and branch right along a small road that leads round the back of the kasbah to its door. Children are likely to come rushing to greet your car and will gladly summon the custodian to unlock the gate and take you on a small tour. This is confined to the most recent portion of the kasbah, including the once magnificent reception rooms and the bower from which the privileged guests of the Glaoui could watch *fantasias* staged for their pleasure in the arena below. Powered by its own electric generator, Telouet had all mod-cons, including a small cinema.

Cinema Epics

Leaving Telouet, return to the Tizi-n-Tichka and proceed to Ouarzazate, a lovely journey following the Asif Imini stream. As the road descends, the landscape and climate become dramatically southern – hot, stony valleys cradling sandcastle *ksour* and palms. Some 32km (20 miles) before Ouarzazate, take a quick look at **Ait-Benhaddou**, 10km (6 miles) off to the left, a picturesque *ksar*, decorated in geometric patterns, that has served as a location for many cinema epics, including scenes in *Lawrence of Arabia, Jesus*

The Glaoui

The Glaoui brothers owed their rapid rise from chiefs of an insignificant mountain tribe to the most powerful men in Morocco to a combination of chance and expedience. Control of the salt mines of the Tizi-n-Telouet Pass, and the perpetual column of caravans that passed to and fro, had made the brothers wealthy. In the winter of 1893, their magnificent hospitality to a war-torn Sultan Moulay Hassan and his rabble army was rewarded by the gift of a Krupp cannon and control of all tribes between the High Atlas and the Sahara. In 1907 Madani el Glaoui (aged 41) was made Grand Vizier and Thami (then 26) was made Pasha of Marrakesh.

In the wake of European encroachment in 1912, the Glaoui sought a pact with the French. In return for greater tax-raising powers they undertook to pacify the tribes of the South, something the French couldn't hope to do on their own. The result was that while the legitimate sultanate was rendered increasingly impotent, the Glaoui brothers, aided by the French, prospered beyond their dreams.

When Madani El Glaoui died, in 1918, Thami took over as chief ally of the French. His lifestyle reflected his political success, and he became a socialite in Europe, giving lavish banquets and priceless presents. He was reputed to be an accomplished and dedicated lover and had talent scouts posted at Morocco's main railway stations to prey upon attractive European woman travelling alone. In 1953 Madani was the personal guest of Winston Churchill, one of his biggest admirers, at the coronation of Queen Elizabeth II at Westminster Abbey, London. This tribal warrior, who a few years before was still mounting the severed heads of enemies on the gates of his kasbahs, had high hopes of returning from London with an English knighthood.

Ultimately, with the rise of the Independence movement and clamours for the reinstatement of Sultan Mohammed V, the French ditched Thami el Glaoui as rapidly as they had once courted him. Soon afterwards, in 1956, the year that Morocco became independent, Thami died from natural causes. He left a family disgraced and dispossessed. His grand kasbahs and palaces fell into ruin, and his servants dispersed. For a while a new word entered the French language, *glaouisé* – betrayed.

of Nazareth and *The Last Temptation of Christ* and, most recently, the provincial town scenes in *Gladiator*, starring Russell Crowe. Park your car in the village and cross the river for a closer look.

Ouarzazate is a modern administrative centre and the springboard for tourism further south. Its only sight is the Taourirt kasbah, another ruined stronghold of the Glaoui, overlooking Barrage el Mansour. (This too has served as a set for films.) Hôtel La Gazelle is on the left side of Avenue Mohammed V as you approach town; Riad Salam is off Mohammed V's eastern end. Dine in the characterful Chez Dimitri (now in the hands of Dimitri's son), also on Avenue Mohammed V, which runs to appetising casseroles and *crêpes Suzette*. Dimitri senior was an energetic Greek, who jumped ship in Casablanca in 1928 as a 14-year-old on his way to the United States. He eventually made his way to the Legionnaire post at Ouarzazate, where he set up his now celebrated restaurant, decorated with souvenirs of the Legion.

The Draa Valley

For those with more time (at least another full day), I strongly recommend the ride south from Ouarzazate to Zagora (168km/104 miles), linking the lush oases of the Draa Valley. Follow the timetable of locals and hit the road in the light of early morning. The extreme beauty of this route unfolds beyond Tizi-n-Tinififft. At **Agdz**, known for its carpets, the road joins the Draa River, thickly flanked by date palms and *ksour*. Take any chance to go inside one of these extraor-

dinary buildings (offering lifts may secure an invitation). Almost all habitation in the valley, animal and human, is concentrated in these fortified *pisé* complexes, reflecting a pre-independence history of almost constant

Above: Aït-Benhaddou. **Right:** upholding family traditions in Chez Dimitri's, Ouarzazate. **Over Page:** the Draa Valley (top) and Agdz (bottom)

feud. Victims of water erosion, *ksour* are rarely more than 100 years old.

To Zagora

Take your time; in the Draa to travel is better than to arrive. Glorious views deserve lengthy contemplation. Aim to reach **Zagora** around noon for a lunch of *brochettes* or *merguez* in one of the cafés on Avenue Mohammed V. Afterwards head on to **Tamegroute** (20 minutes' drive south), the unlikely site of a medieval library containing 13th-century Korans, scientific works and volumes of poetry, prose and mathematics (a guide will show you around). The sand that begins to whip around the wheels hereabouts is an intimation of the *Lawrence of Arabia* landscapes a few kilometres to the south at Tinfou.

After visiting the library, return to Zagora. Either stay the night here (see the italic text at the beginning of this itinerary, if you haven't booked) or meander back up the Draa to Ouarzazate. A recommended extension for those with more time is to cross from the Draa to the Tafilalt Valley – Erfoud and Rissani – via the newly tarmaced road to Tazzarine and Alnif from Tansikht, north of Zagora.

On the following day, return to Marrakesh. Good places for lunch *en route* are Chez Mimi, south of the turning for Telouet on the Tizi-n-Tichka Pass, or Coq Hardi at Pont Du Zak (which is more conveniently placed for those travelling from Ouarzazate). Those who want to move on to Agadir and the Souss, the next section in this guide, should take the N10 west via Taroudannt from Ouarzazate (a fast but comparatively dull stretch of road).

Agadir & the Souss

According to an old Moroccan ballad, 'Nothing ever came from the Souss but oil and lies and locusts'. In fact, historically the Souss, the region south and east of Agadir, is far from being a backwater. It has produced two of Morocco's dynasties, the Almoravides (1071–1147) and the Saadians (1554–1659), and in the early 20th century threw up a serious pretender to the sultanate, El Hiba of Tiznit. In recent decades, the Souss has unleashed nothing more threatening than a legion of *bachal* (cornershop) keepers. Soussi shopkeepers have spread to all corners of Morocco, where they save up for a comfortable retirement in Agadir, the focal city of the Souss, or Tafraoute, an idyllic village deep in the Anti-Atlas.

Agadir is Morocco's principal resort. When the original town, which evolved from a quiet fishing village to a bustling trading port, was razed by an earthquake in 1960, a purpose-built tourist resort was constructed along its impressive bay.

If you are staying in Agadir, it won't take long to find your way around, and because of this we don't include an itinerary of the city itself. Most of the restaurants, hotels, cafés and shops are located along the promenade or sandwiched between Boulevard 20 Août and Boulevard Mohammed V. Worth visiting on a hill at the northern tip of the bay is the 18th-century Kasbah, beneath which the old fishing port is packed with makeshift but appetising seafood restaurants open from late morning until early evening. Other attractions in the city include the Vallée des Oiseaux, a small but well-kept zoo, between Boulevard Mohammed V and Boulevard Hassan II.

Excursions from Agadir

With its immaculate boulevards and gleaming hotel blocks, Agadir is the antithesis of a Moroccan city. Consequently, within a few days you may well be raring to get out and explore *le vrai Maroc*, which in this region is spectacular. This guide recommends two excursions in particular, a circular route through the Anti-Atlas via Tiznit and Tafraoute and a trip to Taroudannt east of Agadir.

An excursion to Marrakesh (273km/ 170 miles) is also highly recommended and possible either on a guided tour (arranged through any travel agency) or independently by car or bus along the N8 (not as interesting as the other mountain passes). Accommodation in Marrakesh must be booked in advance.

Right: Agadir's broad and sandy beach

12. SOUSS AND THE ANTI-ATLAS *(see map below)*

A day-trip from Agadir to the silver centre of Tiznit and through the Anti-Atlas Mountains to the almond-growing town of Tafraoute.

This tour has been designed as a long day-trip, but those with more time to spare could dine and sleep in the 3-star Hotel des Amandiers (tel: 048-800008) in the mountain village of Tafraoute and spend the next day exploring the surrounding villages by foot, either alone or in the company of a local guide. Tafraoute's souk is on Wednesday.

Despite the city's ultra-modern image, Agadir gives several clues to the people's rural roots and its proximity to the desert. It is the only major city where Berber is more commonly spoken than Arabic, and many women are *Sahawri*, their brightly-coloured all-enveloping dress linking them with the women of the Sudan or Somalia rather than the *djellabah*-clad women to the north. These distinctions become increasingly noticeable as you leave Agadir on the N1 to Tiznit (Agadir's main Boulevard Hassan II and Boulevard Mohammed V both feed into this road).

On the way out of town, it is worth stopping at the **Medina d'Agadir** (signposted), a new but traditionally constructed kasbah housing not only handicraft shops but also traditional craft workshops making everything from doors and tesselated tables to mosaic floors for architectural projects thoughout the country.

After passing through a section of the fertile Souss Valley beyond Inezgane, the road crosses 78 dull and dusty kilometres (48 miles) to Tiznit. In summer this road is shrouded in dust; to escape it you might want to branch off to Barrage Youssef Ben-Tachfine and rejoin the N1 at Dehaira, a little outside Tiznit.

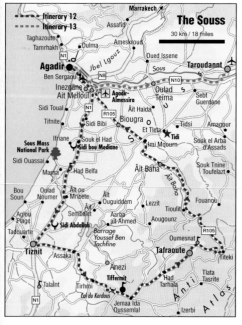

Silver Centre

Tiznit, a typically ochre-coloured, pre-Saharan town, is famous for silver, and a good place to buy both new and antique jewellery. Follow the sign for the medina and enter the city walls through the main gate, known as the Gate of the Three Windows (marked by the Moroccan Star). This leads to the bustling **Place Mechouar**, formerly the parade ground of the French soldiers garrisoned in the town and now packed with buses loading up and setting down. The jewellery souk, Place Kissaria des Bijoutiers, lies behind the side of Place Mechouar opposite Hotel Massaria. There are plenty of shops selling gold items, often worked

Top Right: *zellige* in the making in the Medina d'Agadir
Right: landscape on the way to Tafraoute

in the filigree style popular in the cities, as well as traditional Berber silver jewellery. Among the latter, look out for *khul-khal*, heavy silver anklets, and *fibules*, massive silver brooches used to pin together a woman's overgarment at the shoulders. Common throughout the Berber regions, *fibules* are often in the form of an inverted triangle with a large pin enclosed by a ring. The most impressive examples come from the Tiznit-Tafraoute region, where they are called *tizerzai*.

After taking a look round, have a drink at one of the cafés on the square. It was from here that the pretender El Hiba, known as the Blue Sultan on account of his indigo veil, led 12,000 men on a *jihad* to Marrakesh in 1912, with the promise to rout the Christians and re-establish pure Islam. So powerful was El Hiba's challenge that *caids* (local leaders) went out to meet him to pay homage. The Great Lords who controlled the Atlas passes, Goundafi of the Tizi-n-Test and El Glaoui of Tizi-n-Telouet, tried to hedge their bets, ostensibly supporting El Hiba but covertly colluding with the French. In the end El Hiba's army was massacred, its muskets and powder-flasks being poor defence against French mortars and magazine-rifles.

If you follow Rue de l'Hopital leading off from the square, crossing Place du Pasha, you reach the mosque where El Hiba was acclaimed sultan by the southern tribes. It is quaintly said that the wooden perches on the minaret are designed to assist the dead's ascent to heaven. Carry on north of the mosque to the spring of Lalla Tiznit which, according to legend, miraculously gushed forth when a pious reformed prostitute, Lalla Tiznit, was martyred.

From Tiznit, head east along the R104 to Tafraoute (110km/70 miles), first crossing the stony plain and then twisting up into the hills.

To Tafraoute

From the picturesque oasis of Assaka the road undulates through the foothills of the Anti-Atlas, past pink cube houses and flat-roofed *pisé* villages. It is an extremely pretty route, climbing and winding dramatically past Tirhmi and affording terrific views into valleys of thorny argan trees. The nuts of these trees are popular with tree-climbing goats and the source of a pungent oil used in Berber cooking and believed to be good for the skin.

At **Col du Kerdous**, the Hôtel Kenzi Kerdous (tel: 048-862063), a luxury hotel built in the style of a traditional *ksar*, perches on a rocky pinnacle. It's a good place from which to admire the spectacular views. This remote valley remained staunchly anti-French long after El Hiba's death. At Jemaa Ida Oussemial take the left fork to Tafraoute via Had Tarhala, a route decked in almond blossom in spring.

Tafraoute, the hub of a collection of smaller villages, is hemmed in by massive and seemingly precariously perched boulders. Its extraordinary setting and exhilarating mountain air make it the perfect spot for lunch. Providing a large coach party isn't already installed, adjourn to L'Etoile du Sud, a garden restaurant complete with a caid's tent, which serves good *tajines*. This is the place to meet up with a local guide, your best bet if you want to explore the Tafraoute area on foot. Among other things, he will show you *Les Roches Bleus*, fauvist boulders painted by the Belgian artist Jean Veran. If you are staying overnight, you may want to fix up a hike through the surrounding countryside for the following day.

The road from here to Agadir (150km/92 miles) goes through some of the loveliest scenery in Morocco. It snakes along the high edge of the mountains, with dramatic views above and below. Cone-shaped crops of rock rear out of the valley floor, crowned by *agadirs* (fortified granaries) and farms. Outcrops of palms and white-domed *koubbas* (tombs of holy men) lift the many shades of pink, ginger and brown. As the route is full of bends, leave a good 3 hours before nightfall to complete the return journey. Watch out for pedestrians and livestock: the valley seems remote but is actually densely populated.

Above: Tafraoute
Right: hidden by *haiks*, near Tafroute

13. TAROUDANNT *(see map, page 68)*

An easy day-trip east of Agadir to the ancient city of Taroudannt.

If you are based in Agadir and cannot make it to Marrakesh, it is worth making the shorter trip to Taroudannt (85 km/53 miles east) to sample a traditional walled city with lively souks. By car take the N10 towards Ouarzazate. Buses to Taroudannt leave from Rue Yacoub el-Mansour in the area known as New Talborjt in the northeast district of Agadir.

Surrounded by imposing mud walls, Taroudannt is a miniature Marrakesh. Centuries ago it served as a staging post for dynasties on the road to power, and in the 16th century was a seat of government for the Saadians before the capture of Marrakesh. Later, in 1912, it was also a stronghold of El Hiba, the 'Blue Sultan', whose short-lived revolt against the French protectorate ended in his bloody expulsion at the hands of High Atlas Berbers allied to the colonial power.

Lacking a new town, Taroudannt is mainly contained by its walls. Buses deposit passengers at Bab Zougoun, the southern gate, which is also the point of arrival for drivers from Agadir.

Would-be guides may offer you their services, but these are not strictly neccessary as there are few historic monuments apart from the walls, which still follow their Almoravide plan, and the kasbah. The chief attractions of the town are its souks, north of the central Place el-Alaouyine, the central square, and the tanneries, situated outside the city walls, near Bab Taghount on the west side of town. Smaller but similar to the ones in Fez, the tanneries comprise a network of pits in which the hides are tanned and dyed. Like Fez and Marrakesh, Taroudannt is a good place to buy leather.

Hideaway for the Rich and Famous

About 2km (1 mile) south of town is the esteemed Gazelle d'Or hotel (tel: 048-852039), set in extensive grounds, with a country club atmosphere. Once the home of a French baron, it is one of the most exclusive hotels in Morocco and regularly attracts international celebrities and royalty.

Abve: the ancient walls of Taroudannt

Leisure Activities

SHOPPING

It is unusual to return from Morocco empty-handed. Everywhere you go, the pressure to buy is insistent. Within minutes of your arrival at what may seem to be the most deserted spot on earth a man will pop out of nowhere, open a bag and invite you to 'just have a look'.

You are expected to haggle, and the initial asking price will make allowances for this. Generally, start your bidding at about a third or less of what a vendor asks, but there are no hard and fast rules. Haggling can be prolonged and when larger items are at stake – perhaps a carpet or a leather jacket – it is invariably accompanied by refreshments. If you find yourself enticed into a carpet shop and plied with mint tea, prepare for the hard sell. If you enter a shop in the company of a guide, official or otherwise, you can be certain that he or she will earn commission on what you spend; you won't actually see money exchanging hands – that happens later.

One of the best times to shop is early evening, 5–7pm, when the cool of evening releases a surge of activity in the streets.

Leather

Moroccan leather has long been famous. At one time entire European libraries were sent to Morocco for binding. Nowadays the industry concentrates on leather jackets and bags. In Agadir you can have bespoke leather outfits made within 24 hours for no more than £200 ($300).

One of the most attractive and useful presents to take home is a pair of *babouches*, open-backed slippers (the back is folded down under the heel). They come in an assortment of colours and designs, and women's slippers are often embroidered. For men canary yellow is a popular choice, with white worn on Fridays or special occasions. The Kissaria (traditional shopping mall) next to the Kairouyine Mosque in Fez and the Souk des Babouches in the medina in Marrakesh have the most dazzling selection.

Carpets and textiles

Moroccan carpets are neither as famous nor as fine as those from the Middle and Far East, and are not bought as investments. That said, they can be very striking and difficult to resist. Rabat is the traditional centre for knotted carpets (quality is determined by the number of knots per square centimetre), though Westerners often prefer the flat woven *kilims* of the Middle and High Atlas, with their bold geometrical designs. Different tribes favour different colours and designs, and the museums of popular arts are good places in which to acquire a sense of quality. Marrakesh has a dazzling choice of carpets, though prices are likely to be lower in somewhere like Midelt in the Middle Atlas (a region renowned for weaving).

Less expensive are Berber blankets, often in browns, blacks and creams with geometric designs (buy in the Atlas or Marrakesh). In Tangier and Tetouan you can buy *ftouh*, striking red and white woven wraps worn by women from the Jibali tribes, costing no more than about 40DH.

Also worth considering, but not cheap, is Fez embroidery – usually on table linen and bedspreads – worked in blue, brown or green patterns.

Left: herbalists are hard to resist
Right: a carpet shop, Agadir

Jewellery

If you intend to buy jewellery examine items in a state-run handicraft centre first. Gold, found mainly in the towns, tends to be ornate. 'Hands', to ward off the Evil Eye, are especially popular. The costly gold belts you see on sale are worn by married women at weddings – a gold belt once being an essential part of the bride price. The price of gold jewellery, always weighed, is governed by current gold prices, plus extra for the work.

More chunky, and fashionable in the West, is traditional Berber jewellery. Made of silver and semi-precious stones, it includes heavy bracelets, earrings and elaborate silver pins (*fibules*) the size of door knockers. Tiznit is renowned for its silversmiths and a good place to buy. To help you work out a fair price, bear in mind that in Europe good quality Berber jewellery costs between £60 ($90) for a heavy bracelet and £200 ($300) for one of the massive Berber necklaces. Of course, you should pay a fraction of this, but don't expect items to be dirt cheap.

Pottery

Roadsides are often festooned with pots, plates and bowls. The large serving plates make good buys and survive the change of context when you take them home. Finer examples can be found in the more upmarket shops of Fez. As a rule, ceramic urns etc are not frost-proof, so are unsuitable for Northern European patios in winter.

If you buy a *tajine* pot for use at home, it will need to be seasoned with aromatics and should be used with a heat diffuser.

Spices, cure-alls and perfumes

Apothecaries and spice stalls make fascinating browsing. Among the spices on offer, saffron is a good buy, as is *ras el hanout*, a blend of cumin, ginger, pepper, grains of paradise, cloves, lavender, thyme, rosemary, nutmeg, mace, fenugreek, cinnamon and cardamon. You may want to explore the herbal remedies, too. Many have a sound reputation, but the more esoteric items are for use in outlandish spells and sorcery. Beware Spanish Fly, an aphrodisiac for men made from crushed beetles; it is a urogenital stimulant that can be dangerous.

You will also find perfumeries selling traditional essences, often customised blends. In Tangier, Madini, on Boulevard Pasteur and Rue Sebou (off Rue Ben Raisou, the medina) is renowned. Such places can also reproduce some of the world's most expensive scents.

Woodwork and *Zellige* work

The workshops under the battlements at Essaouira are excellent for woodwork and marquetry, including chess and backgammon sets, salad bowls and low tables.

Zellige (mosaic tilework) has seen a revival in recent years, especially in home furnishings. *Zellige*-topped tables are stunning.

Metalwork

The brass trays and tables that glint at you in every bazaar can look good in the right context, but often look incongruous in a Western setting. The silver-coloured teapots, however, are elegant and capacious.

Gemstones and Fossils

In the mountains, you will see makeshift stalls selling crystals, semi-precious stones and fossils. It was at one such stall that a British mineralogist discovered an entirely new crystal in 1996. Also look out for *rose de sable*, natural sand sculptures that are excavated in the south.

Left: Berber jewellery on display at the Brides' Festival, Imilchil

Le Jardin d'Eau
Boulevard du 20 Août
Tel: 048-840195
Not a bad option for inexpensive Moroccan and French cuisine. Licensed. $–$$

Jazz
Boulevard du 20 Août
Tel: 048-840208
European-style restaurant serving excellent pasta, fish and meat dishes. Licensed. $$

Johara
Boulevard du 20 Août
Tel: 048-845353
The best Moroccan food in town. A lute player provides musical entertainment. $$

Restaurant du Port
Port d'Agadir
Tel: 048-843708
Great fish. Licensed. $–$$

Asilah
Casa Garcia
Rue Moulay Hassan Ben el Mehdi
Tel: 039-417465
Overlooking the harbour, just around the corner from the Bab el Kasaba. This is the best of the fish restaurants in town. Licensed. $$

Casa Pepe
Plaza Zalaka
Tel: 039-417395
Just outside the main gate to the medina. Another good option for fish and shellfish, with several pavement tables. Licensed. $–$$

Casablanca
Casablanca contains numerous good, but generally rather pricey, restaurants, offering a huge variety of cuisines from French and Italian to Vietnamese and Mexican.

A ma Bretagne
Boulevard de la Corniche
Ain Diab
Tel: 022-397979
If you are mobile or prepared to take a longish taxi ride, visit this award-winning restaurant on the corniche south of the Hassan II Mosque, not far from the Marabout of Sidi Abderrahmene. Notable for its superb fish dishes. Ocean views. Licensed. $$$

Al Mounia
Rue du Prince Moulay Abdallah
(off Boulevard de Paris)
Tel: 022-22669
Well-established restaurant specialising in refined Moroccan food. Tasteful belly-dancing also on the menu. Licensed. $$

Le Cabestan
Boulevard de la Corniche
Tel: 022-391190
Well-established and popular French restaurant situated near the lighthouse. Licensed. $$$

Au Petit Rocher
Phare d'El Hank
La Corniche
Tel: 022-366277
Trendy young restaurant and jazz bar on the corniche with a great view of the Hassan II Mosque. Licensed. $$

Restaurant du Port
Through the port entrance
Tel: 022-318561
The place to come for high-quality, good-value fish and seafood. A favourite destination of Casablanca's middle classes. Licensed. $–$$

Royal Mansour Hotel
27 Avenue des FAR
Tel: 022-313011
The hotel's Moroccan restaurant is of a very high quality in a plush setting. Licensed. $$$

Left: Morocco has some of the best fishing grounds in the world

Fez

The medina has a clutch of *dar* type restaurants, particularly in the vicinity of the Kairouyine Mosque. Although the food in such places is reasonable, many are often either packed with tour groups, especially at lunchtime, or empty. Well-heeled *Fassis* tend to prefer the European-style restaurants in the New Town.

L'Anmbra

47 Route d'Immouzer
Tel: 055-541687
A short drive south of the centre on the road to Ifrane, this is Fez's most esteemed restaurant. Famous for Moroccan specialities such as *b'stilla*. It is essential to book and discuss your meal in advance. Licensed. $$$

La Cheminée

6 Avenue Lalla Asma, New Town
Tel: 055- 624902
Well-established restaurant serving quite good French and Moroccan cuisine. Situated close to the railway station. Licensed. $–$$

Chez Vittorio's

21 Rue Brahim Roudani (off Mohammed V)
New Town
Tel: 055- 624730
Long-established restaurant serving good meat and fish as well as first-rate pizzas. Get here by 9pm to be sure of a table. Licensed. $$

Dar Saada

Souk el Attarine, Fez el-Bali
Tel: 055-637370
Situated close to the Kairouyine Mosque, this is a popular choice for tour groups. The food is quite good and the setting palatial. $$

La Maison Bleue

2 Place de L'Istiqal, edge of Fez el-Bali
Tel: 055-741843
Excellent food in an elegant house, near the Musée du Batha, close to the Bab Boujeloud. Traditional musical accompaniment. $$$

Palais Jamai Hotel

Bab Guissa, Fez el-Bali
Tel: 055-634331
The Palais Jamai has a very good formal Moroccan restaurant called Fassia, but it is

Luigi's

Rue Normandie
Tel: 022-940722
Popular high quality Italian restaurant. Tasty pasta, pizza and meat dishes. Licensed. $$

Chaouen (Chefchaouen)

Tissemlal
22 Rue Targui
Tel: 039-986153
Good regional cuisine. No alcohol. $$

Essaouira
Chalet de la Plage

Boulevard Mohammed V
Tel: 044-476419
Perched above the beach. Best for fish but serves other things too. Has a small bar where you can just have a drink with tapas. $$

Chez Sam's

Inside the port
This fish restaurant is something of an institution. Situated inside the port. Licensed. $$

Dar Loubon

24 Rue de Rif
Tel: 044-476296
Imaginative menu combining international and Moroccan influences. Upmarket, but with a bohemian atmosphere. Licensed. $$

Silvestro Pizzeria Ristorante

70 Rue Laalouj
Tel: 044-473555
Good value pizza and pasta restaurant in the medina. Licensed. $$

Above: the subtle use of spices is key to Moroccan cuisine

also worth coming for the hotel's superb lunchtime buffet. Licensed. $$$

Yang-Tse
23 Rue Eritheria, new town
Tel: (055) 621485
A change from Moroccan and international fare, this is a popular Chinese restaurant. $$

Marrakesh

Marrakesh draws wealthy tourists and this is reflected in its choice of fine restaurants, such as Yacout and Tobsil, serving superb food in exquisite surroundings. However, at the other end of the scale, don't be afraid of joining the *Marrakshis* at one of the food stalls on the Jamaa el Fna. Food here – sheep's head (served off the bone), *merguez*, snails in a cumin-flavoured liquor, brochettes, fish, *harira* – is inexpensive and usually very tasty. Each stall is numbered, and the owner's named is posted, so that any complaints can be traced and investigated. For first-rate *merguez*, pull up a chair at Hassan's, No 31.

Al-Fassia
232 Avenue Mohammed V
Tel: 044-434060
Marrakesh's most popular medium priced Moroccan restaurant. Always packed to the rafters. Licensed. $$

Le Cantanzaro
Rue Tarik ibn Ziad
Tel: 044-433731
A good value Italian restaurant/pizzeria. Licensed. $–$$

Casa Lalla
16 Derb Jamaa, medina
Tel: 044-429757
English Michelin two-star chef Richard Neat's newly opened *maison d'hotes*-cum-gastronomic restaurant. There's no menu as such, just inspirational dishes of the day (Moroccan/European) served in a beautiful *riad* in the heart of the medina. Licensed. $$$.

Les Cepages
Faultless service, a convivial environment and reliable French cuisine combine to make this a good option for a quieter evening out in Marrakesh. Licensed. $$–$$$.

Left: grilling *merguez*, spicy lamb sausages

Jad Mahal
Fontaine de la Mamounia Bab Jdid
Tel: 044-436984
Super-chic, hyper-decadent oriental *palais* offering delicious, if expensive, dishes fusing Moroccan and European. Licensed. $$$

Lolo Quoi
82 Avenue Hassan II
Tel: 072-569864
Converted carpet warehouse which serves excellent French and Italian inspired cuisine. Booking essential. Licensed. $$

La Palais Gharnatta
56 Derb el Arfa
Riad Zitoun Jdid, medina
Tel: 044-445218
A family-run restaurant in a traditional *riad* serving first-rate Moroccan cuisine at reasonable prices. Licensed. $$

Le Pavilion
47 Derb Zaouia
Bab Doukala, medina
Tel: 044-387040
Excellent option on the edge of the medina, offering upmarket French cuisine in an attractive, oriental setting. Licensed. $$

Rotisserie de la Paix
68 Rue de la Yougoslavie, Gueliz
Tel 044-433118
Busy restaurant serving a wide range of French and Italian dishes, along with good

grills, fish, shellfish and a few Moroccan dishes. Licensed. $$

Tobsil
22 Derb Moulay Abdellah Ben Houceine
Bab Ksour, medina
Tel: 044-444502
An elegant restaurant, occupying a charmingly restored *riad* (traditional house). Offers a more intimate atmosphere than Yacout, which is of a similar high standard. Highly recommended. Licensed. $$$

Yacout
79 Sidi Ahmed Souss, medina
Tel: 044-382929
Exquisitely decorated and considered one of the best restaurants in Marrakech. Attracts many famous guests. Licensed. $$$

Meknes
Le Dauphin
5 Avenue Mohammed V
Tel: 055-523423
Serving refined French and Moroccan food, plus good seafood. Licensed. $$–$$$

Riad
79 Ksar Chaacha-Dar Kabira
Tel: 055-530542
Lovely garden restaurant serving good Moroccan cuisine. Licensed. $$$

Transatlantique Hotel
Zankat el Meriniyine
Tel: 055-52 00 02
The dining room of Meknes' oldest and best hotel has a good reputation, especially for its Moroccan options. $$–$$$

Zitouna
44 Jemaa Zitouna
Tel: 055-530281
A *dar* restaurant that is used by tour groups, particularly at lunch time. If you want to dine here it is best to call by in advance and discuss your order. Unlicensed. $

Ouarzazate
Restaurant Dimitri
22 Boulevard Mohammed V
Tel: 044-887346
Old French Foreign Legion feel with military memorablia on the walls. Licensed. $$

Ouirgane
La Roseraie
Tel: 044-439128
Luxury hotel on the Tizi 'n-Test Pass through the Atlas. Good restaurant serving international and Moroccan cuisine. Open to non-residents. $$–$$$

Au Sanglier qui Fume
Tel: 044-485707
A roadside auberge serving homely French cooking. Lunch is served on the shady patio in summer. Accommodation available. $$

Rabat
Le Crêpuscule
10 Rue Laghouat (near the cathedral)
Serves tasty *crêpes*. $–$$

Dinarjat
6 Rue Belgnaoui, medina
Tel: 037-704239
Serves first-rate Moroccan food in a beautiful old house. Reserve in advance, and staff will dispatch for a lantern-bearing guide to help you find the restaurant. Licensed. $$$

La Mamma
6 Zekat Tanta (behind Hotel Balima,
off Boulevard Mohammed V)
Good pizzas and Italian food. Always busy,

Above: a corner table in Tobsil, Marrakesh

but they can usually squeeze you in without a reservation. $–$$

Miramar
On the beach at El Harhoura (coast road south of Rabat). Good fish. $

L'Oasis
Place Pietri (off the flower market)
Tel: 037-720557
Moroccan menu and a traditional setting at inexpensive prices. $

La Pagode
13 Rue Baghdad
(behind the railway station)
Tel: 037-763383
For a change of flavours try this well established Chinese restaurant. Licensed. $$

Le Petit Beure – Dar Tajine
8 Rue Damas
Tel: 037-731322
Good quality Moroccan restaurant behind Hotel Balima. Licensed. Closed Sundays. $$

La Plage
Plage Oudaya
Tel: 037-707586
For fish dishes. Situated next to the beach below the Kasbah of the Oudayas. $$–$$$

Tafraoute
L'Etoile du Sud
Tel: 048-8000038
Food is variable but this is the best option in Tafraoute and offers an attractive setting in a *caïd* tent. The house specialities are *tajines*.

Tangier
Tangier's good choice of restaurants is a legacy of its international days. There are also *tapas* bars where, unlike in Spain, the *tapas* are usually free, though type and quantity depend on how much drink is consumed.

El Korsan
El Minzah Hotel
85 Rue de la Liberté
Tel: 039-935885
Tangier's best Moroccan food is found at this sumptuous restaurant in the El Minzah. Licensed. $$$

Guitta's
110 Rue Habib Bourguiba
Tel: 039-937333
Offers al fresco dining in summer and is famous for Sunday lunch. Hard to find as not well signposted. Ring first as opening times are erratic. Licensed. $$

Restaurant Hammadi
2 Rue de la Kasbah
Tel: 039-934514
Kitsch but fun. Moroccan dishes. $

Le Marquis
18 Rue el Bouhtouri
Tel: 039-941132
Upmarket international dining in elegant surroundings. $$

Nautilus
Rue Khalid ibn Walid
Tel: 039-93155
Open in winter only. In summer, visit Nautilus beach café-bar instead.

Osso Bucco
Rue Moulay Abdallah
Italian/international restaurant offering good meat and seafood. Licensed. $$

La Pagode
Rue el Boussouri
Tel: 039-938086
For a first-rate Chinese meal. Popular with expats and wealthy locals. Licensed. $$

San Remo's
15 Rue Ahmed Chaouki
Tel: 039-938451
Well-established, old-fashioned Italian restaurant. Licensed. $$

Near Tangier
Café-Bar Sol
Cap Spartel
Justly popular fish restaurant, a good choice after watching the sunset. Licensed. $$

Restaurant Laachari
Ksar es Seghir (east of Tangier)
A good but unlicensed fish restaurant with a view over the river and ruined fort from its balcony tables. $–$$

NIGHTLIFE

For nightlife, Casablanca has the most sophisticated venues; Rabat, the capital, is fairly staid by comparison. In Agadir and Fez nightlife is mainly confined to nightclubs in the large hotels. Most of them admit non-residents for around 50–150 DH, which usually includes a first drink. They don't generally get going until around midnight.

Agadir

Folklore evenings are laid on in many of the large hotels and often in complexes on the outskirts of town. They may include *fantasias* and Berber singing and dancing.

Casablanca

Casablanca offers the most sophisticated nightlife in Morocco. A new venue seems to open every couple of months, mostly along the Corniche or off the Boulevard Anfa. For a laid-back drink or two try the restaurant-bar Kasbar (7 Rue Najib Mahfound) or for something more up tempo try the Villa Fandango (Rue Mer Egee, Boulevard de la Corniche), one of the best nightclubs. Many other clubs are found at Aïn Diab, the coastal strip south of town, or Mohammedia, on the coast to the north. The number and types of cars parked outside clubs are good indications of their popularity and style.

Marrakesh

In Marrakesh it is hard to beat the nightly entertainment on the Jamaa el Fna; the crowds generally dwindle after about 10pm and the acts disperse, but the Gnaou musicians often keep going until dawn.

For conventional western-style nightlife try the raucous Bodega bar (in Gueliz), or the more refined, though very expensive, bar at Jad Mahal (see restaurant listings). Good nightclubs include the Diamont Noir and the newly-opened Le Pacha which frequently features DJs flown in from Europe for the night. La Mamounia hotel has a piano bar, nightclub (le Club, open from 11pm) and a casino (open from 4pm for slot machines; 8pm for games such as blackjack, roulette and poker.

Tangier

Tangier claims to be the late-night city in Morocco (indeed native *Tanjawis* rarely dine before 10pm) and there is a good choice of idiosyncratic nightlife, which is a legacy from its international days.

Providing you don't expect Ibiza-style trendiness, it's possible to have an enjoyable evening in the city's bars. Among the beach bars on Avenue des FAR, try Emma's bar, Chellah, Golden Beach or, more upmarket, Pasarela or Club 555. In town, try the convivial Tanger Inn, Rue Magellen (in a maze of backstreets running between the corniche and Boulevard Pasteur), which attracts a lively young Moroccan and foreign crowd (no longer particularly gay); the Pub, Rue Soraya; the Wine Bar, Rue Khalil; the Pilo, Rue de Fes; and Casa Ocaña, Rue Rembrandt. Dean's, famous international hangout in the 1950s and '60s, is still operating in Rue Amérique du Sud (off Rue de Liberté), but is now very much a local haunt. At the opposite end of the scale is Le Caid's piano bar in El Minzah hotel, which serves great cocktails.

Among the town's nightclubs are Le Palace in the Hotel Tanjah Flandria; Borsalino, Rue Abdel ben Abdellah; Scott's (gay and straight clientele), Rue el Moutanabi, and the Morocco Palace (Rue du Prince Moulay), which offers kitsch decor, Arab music and, best after midnight, *shikhat* (belly-dancers cum singers).

In 2001 a casino opened in the new Mövenpick Hotel, a short taxi ride along the bay from the centre.

Above: the piano bar in La Mamounia Hotel, Marrakesh

CALENDAR OF EVENTS

Moroccan festivals *(moussems)* tend to revolve around local saints' days, traditional tribal celebrations and harvests, festivals of the cultural kind being recent innovations. The most famous *moussems* attract thousands of visitors and draw itinerant bands of musicians, hawkers, fakirs, storytellers and entertainers. Many include *fantasias*, charging horsemen firing muskets into the air, a tradition with its own festival in Meknes every September.

Big religious *moussems* attract pilgrims from all over Morocco. Moroccans too poor to go on the *haj* to Mecca will make numerous local pilgrimages to compensate.

In addition there are religious festivities linked to the Hegira calendar. Most are celebrated privately in the home, but **Mouloud**, the birthday of the Prophet, is celebrated with candlelit processions in Salé, across the river from Rabat. At **Ashouar**, held 10 days after the onset of the Muslim New Year, children are given presents of sweets and toys. Every evening of Ramadan has an air of festivity, culminating at **Aid-es-Seghi**r, the day after the end of the month-long fast.

January/February
The festival calendar opens with the almond blossom festival in Tafraoute in February, a must for visitors staying in nearby Agadir.

March/April
In March there is a festival of theatre in Casablanca. In April Ouarzazate is the starting point for the week long 'Marathon des Sables' where competitors from around the world run 150 miles through the desert.

May/June
Kelaa des M'Gounna, near Ouarzazate, holds a rose petal festival in May. In June, Sefrou, southeast of Fez, celebrates the cherry harvest, while Asrir near Goulimine in the deep south holds a camel festival. June also sees the *moussem* of Sidi Magdoul in Essaouira.

One of the most important cultural events of the year is the June folklore festival in Marrakesh, when dance troupes and musicians from all over the country perform in the floodlit ruins of El Badi Palace. Fantasias are held every afternoon of the festival.

Right: *fantasias* feature in many festivals

July/August
In July a honey festival is held at Immouzer des Ida Outanane, north of Agadir, while the 'Blue Men's' festival takes place in Goulimine, south of Tiznit. In August the important *moussem* of Moulay Idriss I, the founder of Islam in Morocco, is held in Moulay Idriss, near Fez. On a secular note in August, Asilah, 40km (26 miles) along the coast from Tangier, holds an excellent cultural festival.

September/October
Three important festivals are held in September, the *moussem* of Moulay Idriss II in Fez, when the medina's craftsmen slaughter cattle in honour of the city's patron saint; the *fantasia* festival in Meknes; and the brides' festival in Imilchil (third week of September), when clans of the Aït Haddidou tribe congregate at Imilchil on the Plateau des Lacs in the High Atlas to choose marriage partners. Tourists are welcome and will find makeshift accommodation in 'hotel' tents.

Dates of another kind are celebrated in the southern oases in October, notably in Erfoud, date capital of the Tafilalt. October also sees a music festival in Essaouira.

In September Marrakesh hosts an international film festival where historic sites are turned into cinemas showing new films from around the world. Recent guests include Oliver Stone and Ridley Scott, among others.

November/December
The agricultural fairs draw to a close with olive festivals, notably in Rafsai, the centre of Moroccan olive cultivation, near Fez.

Practical
Information

GETTING THERE

By Air
Morocco's national airline, Royal Air Maroc (RAM), flies from London Heathrow and most of Europe's other principal cities to Tangier, Casablanca (every day from Heathrow), Marrakesh and Agadir. Some flights to Casablanca, Marrakesh and Agadir involve an hour's stop at Tangier. RAM direct flights to Casablanca also operate from Montreal and New York.

Royal Air Maroc
205 Regent Street, London W1
Tel: 020-7439 4361

Royal Air Maroc
75 Sherbrooke Ouest, Montreal,
Quebec H2X 1XZ. Tel: 2851937

Royal Air Maroc
666 Fifth Avenue/at 52nd St, New York, NY 10103, USA. Tel: 974 3850

RAM on the Web:
www.royalairmaroc.com

British Airways has linked up with GB Airways (tel: 020-8877 4000) to run daily flights from London Gatwick to Casablanca and weekly or twice-weekly flights between Gatwick and Tangier, Marrakesh and Agadir and Fez. Royal Air Maroc now offers excellent deals for those who book well in advance through their own low-cost airline Atlas Blue (www.atlas-blue.com).

If you have difficulty finding a cheap flight to Morocco itself, you could fly to Gibraltar and either catch a ferry to Tangier from there (Friday and Monday) or travel into Spain and cross the Strait from Algeciras (a short bus journey away), from where ferries run to Tangier and Ceuta throughout the day (the fare for foot passengers is around 200DH). Alternatively, fly to Málaga and take a coach (2hrs) to Algeciras. Ferries to Morocco also run from Málaga, but these are fewer and the crossing takes 6 hours, and from Tarifa, just west of Algeciras. The Tarifa crossing, served by ferries and hydrofoils, is the shortest of all and involves the least hassle.

Airport/City Links
Most of Morocco's airports connect to the nearest city by taxi (check current rates in the airport information office), but Mohammed V Airport, Casablanca has direct rail links with Casablanca, Rabat and Fez.

By Rail
From Northern Europe the quickest route is via Paris (change from Gard du Nord to Gare Austerlitz) where a direct train leaves for Algeciras at 10.26pm daily. The complete journey will take up to two days. Unfortunately prices do not compare well with flying. Morocco participates in the Inter Rail scheme for young travellers.

By Car
Northern Europe/London to Tangier or Ceuta via Algeciras (the quickest connection from Spain to Morocco) takes up to three days, allowing for overnight stops en route. You could bypass Spain by taking a ferry to Tangier from Sète, near Montpellier, but it is expensive and tedious (36 hours). For details, contact, Southern Ferries, 179 Piccadilly, London W1V 9DB, tel: 020-7491 4968.

Generally, travelling to Morocco by car is expensive, allowing for toll fees in France

Left: passing through Tiznit
Right: a long haul by camel

and Spain as well as ferries (*see page 85 for information*), petrol and overnight accommodation. If possible, avoid travelling in July, when migrant workers clog ports.

For travel through France you will need Green Card Insurance (not necessary for EU members with home country insurance), and for Spain a bail bond, both issued by your regular car insurers. For insurance in Morocco, the best option is to make arrangements when you arrive (see *Assurances aux Frontières* in Tangier's harbour) – your home insurer is unlikely to provide cover. You will also need your vehicle registration document and full driving licence. An international driving licence is not necessary, providing you have a valid national licence. If you want to take a caravan or trailer, consult the Moroccan Tourist Office for advice on the necessary documents.

TRAVEL ESSENTIALS

When to Go

Good general times to go are spring (April/ May, even early June), when the scenery is enhanced by wild flowers and the melted snows of the Atlas Mountains augment rivers and streams, or late September and early October, when the heat has mellowed and date harvests are in full swing. All regions are then comfortably warm. That said, try to avoid Easter, when Morocco is inundated by Spaniards escaping Semana Santa. Ramadan, the month-long time of fasting (governed by the Hegira calendar and therefore moveable), has some disadvantages for the independent traveller, not least the fact that many cafés and restaurants outside Agadir and large hotels are closed during the day or sometimes for the whole month.

Marrakesh is always busy, even in high summer, so it is essential to book your accommodation here in advance.

Visas and Passports

Full EU, Australian, Canadian, US and New Zealand passport holders do not require visas and are normally granted entry for a maximum of 90 days. Temporary passports are not accepted.

Vaccinations

Unless you are arriving from a declared infected zone, no inoculations are required by Moroccan law. Cautious doctors advise precautions against typhoid, polio, cholera and tetanus. If you are travelling through the south in summer a course of anti-malarial pills is recommended.

Customs

Duty-free allowances for visitors to Morocco are: 200 cigarettes or 50 cigars; either 75 cl spirits and 1 bottle of wine or 3 bottles of wine; ¼ litre of *eau de cologne*. If you arrive by ferry or a scheduled flight, you'll find that customs officers are more concerned about searching the baggage of returning Moroccans than that of tourists.

The import and export of Moroccan dirhams is forbidden. Visitors can import as much foreign currency as they wish.

Selling imported cars or other high-value goods is an offence. Any such item noted in your passport on arrival must be taken out of Morocco at the end of your stay.

Climate

As a rule, coastal regions have warm dry summers and mild, damp winters, though Agadir and south of Agadir, free of Atlantic depressions and sheltered by moutains, tend to be warm and dry all year round. The Atlantic is a welcome cooling factor on the coast, though the effect of cold and warm air meeting can produce mists, particularly between El Jadida and Agadir.

Apart from the High Atlas region, which is cooled by altitude, inland Morocco is ferociously hot in summer. In August Fez has an average daily maximum temperature of 36°C; Marrakesh, 37°C; and Ouarzazate 40°C (96°, 98° and 104°F respectively). Sometimes these temperatures climb far higher. Summer temperatures in Tangier average 27°C (80°F), but here you need to watch out for the *chergui*, a pesky east wind. Winter temperatures include a comfortable 19/20°C (68°F) in Agadir, Marrakesh and Ouarzazate, falling to an average daytime temperature of 15°C (59°F) in Tangier and Fez (where rain is likely). Temperatures drop severely at night in winter, so come prepared.

Winter travel through the Middle and High Atlas can be curtailed by snowfalls and in early spring or late autumn roads are sometimes closed because of flash floods. If you are touring Morocco during tempestuous weather expect to make changes to planned routes.

Electricity

Most of the country's supply is rated 220 volts, but a few places still have a 110 volt supply; sockets and plugs are of the continental variety, with two round pins, so you will need to take an adaptor.

Time Difference

Morocco sticks to Greenwich Mean Time all year round. This means that in summer it is usually an hour behind the UK and two hours behind the rest of Europe. In winter it keeps the same time as the UK.

GETTING ACQUAINTED

Religion

Morocco is a comparatively tolerant Muslim country, but religion is still the biggest influence on society. The five requirements of Islam – affirmation that there is no other god but God and Mohammed is his Prophet; prayer five times a day; the observance of Ramadan; the giving of alms to the poor; making the *hadj* (pilgrimage) to Mecca at least once in a lifetime – are central to many Moroccan lives. If you doubt it, come to Morocco during Ramadan; the solidarity that the daily fast engenders is impressive.

A solid grounding in the Koran, believed to be the direct word of God revealed to his Prophet Mohammed – is regarded as the best guide to life there is. Many young children attend a religious kindergarten where they learn the Koran's verses by rote.

Officially Morocco follows the Sunni (orthodox) branch of Islam. However, there are a number of thriving Sufi brotherhoods, which promote a more mystical approach to God, aiming to achieve religious experience through trance and ecstatic rituals. Some of their practices, including self-mutilation in the case of the more extreme Sufi sects, such as the Assouia and Hamadasha based in Meknes, have now been outlawed. Paul Bowles' novel *The Spider's House* contains compelling accounts of such sects.

In addition, Moroccan Islam contains a strong pantheistic streak stemming from ancient Berber beliefs. It is common, for example, for rural Moroccans, women in particular, to pay homage to trees and streams reputed to be sacred. Many of the white-domed *koubba* (tombs of holy men) that you see dotted on hillsides and on coastal headlands are places of pilgrimage.

How Not to Offend

As Morocco is an Islamic country, albeit a fairly liberal one, women shouldn't sunbathe topless and no one should swim nude, even in remote mountain streams. If you go to a *hammam*, it is customary to retain your underpants. It is polite to dress fairly discreetly in towns.

As a guest in a Moroccan home, follow two rules: never take alcohol as a gift (a box of pastries is usually a welcome offering)

Left: cover up to escape the heat
Right: *koubbas* (tombs of a holy men) are often places of pilgrimage

and offer to remove your shoes before venturing on the carpets. The usual practice at meal-time is for everyone to eat from one central bowl, using bread or their right hand to scoop up the food. The host will often break off particularly succulent pieces of meat and offer them to more reticent guests.

In Ramadan, one should refrain from eating, smoking or displays of physical affection in public during daylight hours. A

Moroccan doing any of these things in Ramadan could be thrown in jail, so such action by a foreigner is bound to offend.

Taking photographs, particularly in rural areas, is another source of misunderstanding. Although some people are keen to encourage photographs, especially if they can make a few dirhams out of it, others are not. A belief persists among older Berbers that a camera has the power to snatch souls (Michel Tournier's novel *The Golden Droplet*, set in Algeria, explores this theme). Desist if your subject starts waving his or her arms around; better still, ask first.

Whom Do You Trust?

The late Paul Bowles claimed that it was almost impossible to have a genuine friendship with a Moroccan. This isn't true, but it is easy to get that impression on the basis of the sort of Moroccans that tend to approach tourists – the *faux-guides*, whose

main aim is to lure foreigners into the bazaars and earn commission on what they spend. In recent years, following regular criticism in the foreign press, the Moroccan government has made a concerted effort to clamp down on the problem. However, in a country with high unemployment and no state benefits it is likely to re-emerge. If you become a victim, be firm and try to keep your sense of humour; dealing with the worst *faux-guides* can be a psychological war. Once past the gates of a medina, where many of them hang out, it is usually possible to proceed unpestered. If you get lost, don't hesitate to ask a local for help. The vast majority of Moroccans are extremely helpful.

Many official guides, hired from the tourist office, are also keen to earn commission in the bazaars. If you are not interested in buying, it is best to point this out before setting off on a tour.

Beware a friendship struck up over hashish or *kif*. It may be a set-up. If the police arrive, you may have to bribe your way off the hook – which is an offence in itself.

MONEY MATTERS

The Moroccan dirham is divided into 100 centimes. Recent exchange rates are 15 DH to £1; 10 DH to $1.

Travellers' cheques are one of the safest ways of carrying money. If lost or stolen they can be replaced. However, not all banks will change them; two which do are BMCE and Atijariwafa Bank, and commission is nominal. If you are entering Morocco outside normal banking hours it is useful to have some cash.

Remember that banks are closed over the weekends and on public holidays. *Bureaux de change* in large hotels usually offer a less favourable rate of exchange.

Most better restaurants and hotels now take credit cards, as do some shops. The most popular are Visa, Carte Bleu, American Express and Eurocard, but Mastercard is quickly gaining ground. The number of ATMs is rapidly increasing but they remain rare outside the larger towns.

You are not supposed to take Moroccan money out of the country. You can convert

Above: an official guide shows his credentials

unwanted Dirhams back into hard currency, but only at the exchange kiosk at an airport, and you must be able to show exchange receipts totalling twice the amount you wish to exchange.

GETTING AROUND

Taxis

Grand-taxis, usually Mercedes, are shared taxis which travel from town to town. They are inexpensive (only slightly more than a seat on a bus) and fast. *Petit-taxis* cannot go beyond city limits or take more than three passengers. They are cheap and handy, and most have a working meter.

For travel to and from an airport, you must hire one of the Mercedes taxis, which are a lot more expensive when hired individually.

Train

Morocco's railway (ONCF) connects Tangier, Rabat, Casablanca, Fez, Oujda and Marrakesh and towns en route. It doesn't extend south of Marrakesh. Second-class carriages on autorail trains are air-conditioned and comfortable. Rail travel costs slightly more than bus. For information in advance of your visit, including fares and timetables, contact the ONCF website: www.oncf.org.ma.

Bus

Buses are a good way of getting to more remote areas. The national company, CTM, has air-conditioned coaches (CTM stations are often separate from the main bus station). Scores of cheaper, privately-owned companies run a more basic service.

By Car

Hiring a car is expensive. If tourism is busy (high summer in Tangier and Agadir; Easter everywhere; and autumn through spring in Marrakesh and the south) it can work out cheaper to hire in advance of your stay through a company such as Budget or Europcar. Out of season, it may be worth hiring locally and haggling over the price, particularly for periods of two weeks or more.

Whether the car is your own or hired, keep documents – licence and log book – handy to show *gendarmes*, who stop motorists fre-

Right: petrol stations are plentiful along main highways

quently, especially at major junctions or on the outskirts of towns. Infringement of the law – speeding, etc – can mean an on-the-spot fine. Speed limits are 40kph (25mph) in urban areas, 100kph (60mph) on the open road and 120kph (74mph) on the motorways between Casablanca and just north of Larache and between Rabat/Casablanca and Fez (but look out for signs specifying other limits). The French system of *priorité a droite* (priority to the right) operates. This means that traffic engaged on a roundabout must give way to traffic coming on to the roundabout unless otherwise indicated.

Wherever you park in Morocco, there will be a *gardien* (attendant), though much of Casablanca has meters. Two or three dirhams is sufficient for an hour or two, but overnight parking costs around 10 DH. Most large cities now have petrol stations selling lead-free *(sans plomb)*.

HOURS & HOLIDAYS

Business Hours

Banks open: winter Mon–Fri 8.30–11.30am and 2.30–4pm; summer Mon–Fri 8.30am–11.30am and 3–5pm; and during Ramadan Mon–Fri 9.30am–3pm. These are the official opening times, but it is best to check locally as there are regional differences.

Post offices open 8.30am–noon and 2.30–6.30pm (only until noon on Saturday). Museums and sites vary, but expect to find them open 9am–noon and 3–6pm (some close on Tuesdays; and some *madrassas* close on Friday morning).

Shops tend to vary, but generally close for 2–4 hours from midday; they make up for this by staying open until 8 or 9pm.

Business hours change during Ramadan.

Public Holidays
State holidays
1 Janauary, New Year's Day
11 January, Independence manifesto.
1 May, Labour Day.
30 July, Feast of the Throne.
14 August Allegiance of Wadi-Eddahab.
20 August, anniversary of the King's and people's revolution.
21 August, Youth Day.
6 November, anniversary of the Green March.
18 November, Independence Day.
Religious holidays (governed by the Hegira calendar, which is lunar and therefore moveable).
Aid es Seghir (day after the end of Ramadan).
Aid el Kebir (feast of the lamb), in honour of Abraham's sacrifice of his son, when some 4 million sheep are sacrificed.
Muslim New Year.
Mouloud (birthday of the Prophet).

Market Days
The name of a village or town often reflects the day of its weekly souk: el Had (Sunday); el Tnine (Monday); el Telata (Tuesday); el Arba (Wednesday); el Khemis (Thursday); el Djemna (Friday); es Sebt (Saturday). Thus Souk el Arba (on the Tangier–Rabat road) holds its souk on Wednesday.

Heavy traffic of mules and people in rural areas is a sign that there is a souk close by, as is a large encampment of tents.

ACCOMMODATION

Hotel categories range from unclassified (generally basic establishments) to 5-star de luxe. Prices are always posted in the reception area. Approximate prices for a double room are: 5-star 1,200–2,500DH; 4-star 600–1,200DH; 3-star 300–600DH; 2-star 200–300DH, 1 star 150–200DH.

Agadir
Most of Agadir's city hotels are strung out along Boulevard 20 Août and Boulevard Mohammed V. In summer, most of these are filled by groups. New hotels are also being built on the Inezgane road south of the city.

Sofitel Agadir (5 star)
Cite Founty P4
Tel: 048-820088
Vast luxury resort hotel right on the beach. The best hotel of its kind in Agadir.

Hotel Riu Tikida Beach (4-star)
Chemin des Dunes
Tel: 048-845400; Fax: 048-842221
Huge oceanside hotel with a private beach, numerous activities and a health spa.

Hotel Miramar (3-star)
Boulevard Mohammed V
Tel: 048-840770; Fax: 048-840770
Small comfortable hotel overlooking the beach near the port. Popular restaurant. No pool. Rear rooms are quieter.

Asilah
Hotel Patio de la Luna (3-star prices)
12 Plaza Zelaka
Tel: 039-416074
Charming eight-room *maison d'hotes* located just outside Bab Kasaba. Small but nicely decorated rooms with en-suite facilities.

Casablanca
Royal Mansour Meridien (5-star)
27 Avenue des FAR
Tel: 022-313011;
Fax:022-314818
www.lemeridien-casablanca.com
Luxurious, with a good central position and a lot more character than the city's other top hotels. However, there is no pool.

Left: a souk in full swing

Hyatt Regency (5-star)
Place des Nations Unies
Tel: 022-431234; Fax:022-431334
Long-established hotel in the heart of town, just outside the main gate of the medina. Good amenities, including pool.

Ibis Moussafir (3-star)
Place de la Gare
Tel: 022-401984; Fax:022-400799
Situated next to Casa-Voyageurs railway station. Modest but comfortable accommodation representing good value. No pool.

Hotel de Noailles (2-star)
22 Boulevard du 11 Janvier
Tel: 022-202554; Fax: 022-220589
A good, centrally-located option. Some rooms have terraces.

Chaouen (Chefchaouen)
Parador (4-star)
Place el Makhzen
Tel: 039-986324; Fax: 039-987033
Situated at the top of the town, with views over the valley. Well-run, comfortable, with pool in summer.

Hostel Gernika (unclassified)
49 Rue Onssar
Tel: 039-987434
Run by an artistic Spanish woman. Spotlessly clean with a pretty terrace.

Essaouira
Heure Bleue (5-star)
2 Rue Ibn Batuta
Tel: 044-783434
www.heure-bleue.com
Essaouira's premier hotel located just inside the city wall at Bab Marrakesh. Luxuriously converted, the hotel offers lavish rooms, a spa and great views from its rooftop pool.

Villa Maroc
10 Rue Abdellah ben Yassin
Tel: 044-476147; Fax:044-475806
www.villamaroc.com
Stylish, comfortable hotel in 18th-century house built into the ramparts. Moroccan meals cooked to order. Open fires out of season. Prices are above average but worth it.

Riad al Madina
9 rue Attarine
Tel: 044-475907; Fax: 044-475727
www.riadalmadina.com
Medium-priced hotel, with traditionally furnished rooms set around a central courtyard.

Tafoukt
Boulevard Mohammed V
Tel 044-784504; Fax 044-784505
Basic but very clean, with sea view.

Fez
The hotel you choose will partly depend on whether you want to be close to Fez el-Bali or prefer to be in the New Town, which is livelier in the evening. You may want access to a pool in summer, when Fez gets very hot. With advance planning, you could also consider renting a *riad* (traditional house) in the medina; contact www.fesmedina.com.

Sofitel Palais Jamai (5-star)
Bab Guissa
Tel: 055-635331; Fax: 055- 635096
Converted palace, with lovely gardens, on the edge of Fez el-Bali. Its medina-facing rooms have the best views in town. Notable restaurant. Recently renovated.

Maison Bleue *(maison d'hote)*
2 Place de L'Istiqal, Fez el-Bali
Tel: 055-636052; Fax: 055-40686
www.maisonbleue.com

Above: a hotel with a pool is recommended in summer

Beautiful family-owned hotel occupying a former palace on the edge of Fez el-Bali. Has one of the best restaurants in Fez.

Hotel Menzeh Zalagh (4-star)
Rue Mohammed Diouri, New Town
Tel: 055-625531; Fax: 055-651995
Well-run busy hotel, with pool, garden and views over to Fez Jdid. When booking, specify the original Menzeh Zalagh and not the more functional Zalagh 2, down the road.

Hotel Ibis Moussafir (3-star)
Plaza de la Estacion, New Town
Tel: 055-651902; Fax: 055-651909
Next to the railway station. Functional but comfortable, with pool, garden and restaurant.

Hotel Splendid (3-star)
9 Rue Abdelkrim el Khattabi, New Town
Tel: 055-622148; Fax: 055- 654892
Air-conditioning in the rooms, though these are otherwise fairly basic. Pool and bar.

Hotel Amor (2-star)
31 Rue Arabie saoudite
Tel: 055-622724
Good budget option near the station. Private facilities. Bar. Rooms can be hot in summer.

Hotel Batha (2-star)
Place al Batha, Fez el-Bali
Tel: 055-634824; Fax: 055-741078
This small hotel has a good position near Bab Boujeloud. Rooms are attractive (set around a courtyard) and there is a pool. 3-star prices.

Marrakesh

There are many hotels at all price levels in Marrakesh, but not enough to accommodate the ever-growing number of visitors, therefore independent travellers are strongly advised to book in advance. When considering a hotel, decide whether you want to stay in or near the medina or in Gueliz, the new town. Hivernage, between the medina and Gueliz is quite a popular area.

As an alternative to staying in a hotel, you may want to consider staying in a *riad*, a traditional Moroccan house that can be rented by the day, week or month. Some of these have been beautifully restored, and often come with a housekeeper or cook. Several agencies specialise in renting and selling *riads*, including Marrakech Medina (www.medina-marrakech.com).

Amanjena (5-star deluxe)
Route de Ouarzazate, city outskirts
Tel: 044-403353; Fax: 044-403477
The first Amanresort in Africa, Amanjena is the ultimate in luxury, costing a minimum $700 dollars a night (half the average annual wage in Morocco). Guests are accommodated in palatial private pavilions set among palm and olive trees. Superb cuisine, fabulous beauty centre and an 18-hole golf course are among the many amenities.

Above: one of many similar options in the resort of Agadir

practical information

La Mamounia (5-star deluxe)
Avenue Bab Jdid, near medina
Tel: 044-444409; Fax: (044) 444910
www.mamounia.com
Occupying a former palace, this is one of the world's great hotels and as such it attracts the rich and famous. Winston Churchill stayed here. Beautiful gardens, every amenity.

Villa des Orangers (5 star)
6 Rue Sidi Mimoune
Tel: 044-384638
Fax: 044-385123
www.villadesorangers.com
Relais & Châteaux hotel close to the gates of the royal palace. A beautifully restored *riad* with two pools, luxurious bedrooms and bathrooms and an excellent Moroccan restaurant.

Grand Imilchil (3-star)
Avenue Echouhada, Hivernage area
Tel: 044-447653; Fax:044-446165
A good-value hotel with pool and large rooms, situated near the medina. Restaurant, no bar.

Hotel Nassim (3-star)
115 Avenue Mohammed V, Gueliz
Tel: 044-446401; Fax: 044-436710
Well-run hotel in the heart of Gueliz, with cosy bar and a small pool.

Hotel Sherazade (unclassified)
Derb Riad Zitoune, medina
Tel/Fax: 044-429305
Popular small hotel with good rooftop terraces offering views of the Koutoubia.

Hotel Gallia (2-star)
Rue de la Recette, edge of medina
Tel: 044-445913; Fax: 044-444853
Spotless hotel. Breakfast served in courtyard.

Hotel Ali (unclassified)
Rue Moulay Ismail, medina
Tel: 044-444979
Popular amongst backpackers. Quite a decent restaurant on the terrace in summer.

Meknes
Hotel Transatlantique (4-star)
Zankat el Merinyine
Tel: 055-525050; Fax: 055-520057
transat@iam.net.ma
Long-established luxury hotel, with excellent restaurant, lovely gardens and views over the medina.

Hotel Rif (4-star)
Rue d'Accra
Tel: 055-522591; 055-524428
Comfortable hotel, with flamboyant decor. Swimming pool. Situated in the new town.

Bab Mansour (3-star)
38 Rue Emir Abdelkader
Tel: 055-525239; Fax: 055-510741
Well-run medium-size hotel with good facilities including bar and restaurant.

Hotel Majestic (2-star)
19 Avenue Mohammed V
Tel: 055-522035
Good value hotel with a touch of character in the *ville nouvelle*. Large bedrooms, most with private bathroom, but avoid noisy rooms at the back of the hotel (facing the railway station).

Hotel Volubilis (1-star)
45 Avenue des FAR
Tel: 055-525082
Good medium-range option, with bar and cabaret.

Meknes Region
Tijania Range
El Menzeh road, south of Meknes
Tel: 067-820373
In the heart of Meknes' vineyards, this Arabian stud farm, organic farm and country restaurant also has rooms.

Above: through the keyhole arch, La Mamounia, Marrakesh

Rabat
La Tour Hassan (5-star)
26 Rue Chellah BP 14
Tel: 037-239000; Fax: 037-725408
Classiest of the luxury hotels, with a good position overlooking the river, near the Tour Hassan. Amenities include a pool.

Hotel Helnan Chellah (4-star)
2 Rue d'Ifni
Tel: 037-668300; Fax: 037-706354
Pleasant modern hotel in quiet location near the archaeological museum at the southern end of town. No pool.

Hotel Balima (3-star)
Avenue Mohammmed V
Tel: 037-707755; Fax: 037-707450
Old hotel opposite the parliament building on the main boulevard and not far from the station. Recently refurbished. Large rooms.

Hotel Majestic (2-star)
121 Avenue Hassan II
Tel: 037-722997
Friendly hotel overlooking Bab el Had. Rooms have TV and private bathroom.

Tangier
Hotel el Minzah (5-star)
85 Rue de la Liberté
Tel: 039-935885; Fax: 039-934546
www.elminzah.com
Refined Moorish decor, good restaurants, secluded garden, pool and spa. Central position. Rooms to the rear have sea views.

Hotel Solazur (4-star)
Avenue des FAR
Tel: 039-320759; Fax: 039-945286
Large and popular package-market hotel overlooking the beach. Pool.

Hotel Rembrandt (3-star)
Avenue Mohammed V
Tel: 039-333314; Fax: 039-930443
Elegant older-style hotel that has been recently renovated. Central position.

Hotel Chellah (3-star)
Rue Alal ben Abdellah
Tel: 039-321002; Fax: 039-320998
Central, popular hotel, with pool.

Hotel Continental (2-star)
36 Rue Dar Baroud
Tel: 039-931024; Fax: 039-931143
Faded grand hotel situated just below the Kasbah and above the port.

Hotel Ibn Batouta (2-star)
8 Rue Magellan
Tel: 039-939311; Fax: 039-939368
Attractive, well-run hotel in a steep back street between the corniche and Boulevard Pasteur. It is very close to a mosque, but you get used to the early morning call to prayer.

Hotel El Muniria (unclassified)
1 Rue Magellan
Tel: 039-935337
This good value hotel was a popular hangout of writers and artists in the 1950s and '60s. Most rooms have showers. There is a lively, if a little dowdy, bar, below the hotel.

HEALTH & EMERGENCIES

Emergency Telephone Numbers
Police **19**
Fire service/Ambulance **15**

Water and Hygiene
Tap water in cities is safe, but elsewhere it is best to stick to bottled water – usually Sidi

Right: many rural villagers still draw their water from wells

Harazem or Oulmes. Swim only in rivers or mountain pools with clear, fast-flowing water; bilharzia may be lurking. The greatest health threat is contaminated food. Choose restaurants where the meat, often on display, looks fresh and trade is brisk. If you have a stomach upset, drink plenty of bottled water and try a local remedy – peeled cactus fruits, sold from barrows on street corners. In cases of diarrhoea or vomiting, replace body salts by using a rehydration solution, available at pharmacies. The latter are plentiful, with helpful staff; antibiotics are available over the counter.

Medical/Dental Services

All medical aid must be paid for, so take medical insurance that includes repatriation, if necessary. A pharmacist will be able to direct you to a local doctor or dentist. Keep receipts.

Crime and the Police

By international standards, petty theft is not particularly common. That said, take sensible precautions. Never leave valuables unattended and keep a tight hold on bags in the medinas. Avoid wearing jewellery or carrying a lot of money, and use safe deposit boxes in hotels. If you have a car, park it where an attendant can keep an eye on it, especially at night.

If you suffer theft or loss, report it to the police and insist on receiving a record of the report – even if it is only a stamped piece of paper – for insurance purposes.

If you bring your own car into the country, inspect it before leaving to ensure hashish has not been stowed inside or underneath.

Police are responsible for urban areas, and *gendarmes* (generally riding motorcycles) are responsible for rural areas. *Gendarmes* and customs officer frequently flag down vehicles to examine papers, etc. Make sure you keep your papers with you at all times. Watch out for speed traps on city approach roads.

COMMUNICATIONS & NEWS

Post

Post-boxes are yellow. The postal system is unpredictable, postcards and letters taking anything from four days to four weeks to reach international destinations.

Right: no shortage of reading matter

Telephone

International calls are possible from public telephone booths (some take 5 DH coins and some phone cards, available from post offices and some grocery stores), and also from PTT (Poste, Telegraphe et Telephone) offices, or from one of the many *telebou-tiques*. The latter are always clean and usually have someone on duty to supply change.

Dial 00 for an international line, followed by the national code (44 for the UK; 1 for Canada and the US; 61 for Australia; 64 for New Zealand; 31 for the Netherlands, 34 for Spain; 49 for Germany) and then the number you wish to dial, minus any initial zeros. Local codes are normally posted in phone booths.

E-mail

Internet cafés abound. Internet access costs from just 10 DH an hour.

Newspapers

Several Moroccan papers are published in French, the most popular being *L'Opinion* and the strongly royalist *Le Matin*. Weeklies include *Le Journal* and *Gazette du Maroc*. European papers are widely available, as are French (and some English) magazines.

Radio and Television

There are two Moroccan channels, TVM and the more interesting 2M (both state run, though the latter has more independence). MBC (Middle Eastern Broadcasting Corporation), broadcast from London, is also available, as is the French-backed Medi-1, which operates radio and television broadcasts from Tangier. In the north, Spanish and Portuguese channels can be picked up, as can Gibraltar television (BBC1) in the north providing you have the receiver. Satellite television is inexpensive and widespread.

LANGUAGE

Spoken languages are primarily Moroccan Arabic, French and Berber dialects, with the addition of English in Tangier and Spanish in the north as a whole. Moroccans working in tourism tend to speak several European languages. If you speak some French, you will have no difficulty making yourself understood.

General

Hello *Márhaba, ahlan*
Greetings *As-Salám aláykum* (peace be with you), reply *Waláykum as-salam* (and to you peace)
Welcome *Ahlan wasáhlan*
Good morning *Sabáh el-Kháyr*
Good evening *Masá el-kháyr*
Goodbye *Máa Saláma*
How are you? *Lebass/káyf hálak* (to a man)/
Káyf hálik (to a woman)
Well, fine *Al-hámdu li-llá*
Please *min fádlak*
Thank you *Shúkran*
Thanks be to God *Al-hámdu li-lla*
Yes *Náam* or *áiwa*
What is your name? *Sh'nu ismik?* (to a man)/
Sh'nnu ismak (to a woman)
My name is... *Ismi...*
Where are you from? *Min wáybn inta?*
(for a man)/*Min wáyn inti?* (for a woman)
I am from England *Ana min Ingílatra*
I am from the United States *Ana min Amérika*
Do you speak English? *Tkellem Inglesa?*
Do you speak French? *Tkelem Fransáwi?*
I do not understand *Ma báfham*
What does this mean? *Shka te ani?*
Never mind *Ma'alésh*
It is forbidden *Mamnú a*
What time is it? *Adáysh as-sáa*

Food and Drink

fish *sámak*
meat *láhma*
milk *halíb*
bread *khúbz*
salad *saláta*
coffee *káhwa*
tea *shái*
with sugar *bi súkkar*
without sugar *bla súkkar*

wine *sh'rab*
beer *bíra*
mineral water *mái ma'adaniya*
I am a vegetarian *Ana nabbáti* (for a man)/
nabbatiya (for a woman)
the bill *el-hisáb*

Shopping

market *souk*
money *fulús*
cheap *rakhís*
expensive *gháli*
receipt *fatúra*
How much does it cost? *Adáysh?/bi-kam?*
What would you like *Sh'nou khsek?*
I like this *Baghi hádha*
I do not like this *Ma baghish hádha*
How many? *Kam?*

Hotel

How much does a room cost per night?
Sha'al al bit allayla?
a free room *ghúrfa fádia*
single room *ghúrfa munfárida*
double room *ghúrfa musdáwija*
shower *dúsh*
towel *foota*

Emergencies

I need help *bídi musáada*
doctor *doct*
hospital *mustáshfa*
pharmacy *saidalíya*
I am sick *Ana marídh* (for a man)/
Ana marídha (for a woman)
diarrhoea *ishál*
police *shúrta*
lawyer *muhámmi*

Transport

Where..? *Wáyn...?*
downtown *wást al bálad*
taxi *táxi*

Above Right: one message, three languages

shared taxi *servís*
aeroplane *tayára*
station *mahátta*
to *íla*
from *min*
right *yamín*
left *shimál*
street *shária*

Glossary

agadir fortified granary
agdal garden
Aid el Kebir feast day celebrating Abraham's Sacrifice of the Lamb
Aid es Seghir feast day held after the first sighting of the moon after Ramadan
El Andalus Muslim Spain
bab gate
baraka blessing, often thought magical
bled el makhzen land of government
bled es siba land of dissidence
Caid district judge
Jemma assembly, but also mosque
jinn spirit
fondouk lodging house with stables
Hadith the written traditions of Islam
Haj the pilgrimage to Mecca
hammam steam bath
horm sanctuary
imam prayer leader
jebel mountain
koubba white, domed building containing the tomb of a saint
ksar (ksour) fortified *pisé* building or community (plural)
l'tam veil
Maghreb collective name for Morocco, Algeria and Tunisia
makhzen government
marabout saint
mechouar square, assembly area
madrassa Islamic college
medina old town
mellah Jewish quarter
mihrab niche indicating direction of Mecca in mosque
minaret tower of mosque
moujehaddin Islamic soldiers engaged in Holy war
Moulay indicates descendancy from the Prophet
Mouloud Prophet's birthday
moussem religious festival

musezzin caller to prayer
oued river
shouaf fortune teller
tizi mountain pass
zaouia religious fraternity
zellige tile mosaics

SPORT & ACTIVITIES

Golf

Thanks to King Hassan II, who was a keen golfer, golf has a long history in Morocco and has received a lot of investment. The best course is **Rabat's** Royal Dar-Es-Salam, designed by Robert Trent Jones (tel: 037-755864; fax: 037-757671), where the Moroccan Open and the Hassan II trophy are held: 45 holes, Red (18), Blue (18), Green (9).

Marrakesh has three courses, the 18-hole Royal Golf Club (tel: 044-444341; fax: 044-400084) and, just opposite, Club Amelkis, 18-holes (tel: 044-404414), which lies within the Amanjena complex. The third course is the 18-hole Golf de la Palmeraie, (part of the Palmeraie Golf Palace Resort) designed by Robert Trent Jones (tel: 044-301010).

Other courses include **Mohammedia**, north of Casablanca: 18 holes (tel: 023-324656; fax: 023-321102); **Tangier**: 18 holes (tel: 039-938925; fax: 039-939025); **Cabo Negro** (tel: 039-978141), a 9-hole course near Tetouan; **Ouarzazate** (tel: 044-882216), a 9-hole course due to be extended to 18 holes; and the 9-hole course at **Meknes** (tel: 055-530753; fax: 055-557934). **Agadir** has three courses: the Club Med Dunes Club (three 9-hole courses; tel: 048-834547), the Golf du Soleil (9 and 18 holes; tel: 048-337329) and the 9-hole Royal Agadir

Right: traditional desert transport

ited guides and as well as detailing the prices for mules and other mountain services.

Biking and Rafting

In the wake of increased interest in hiking holidays in the Atlas, travel companies are expanding into mountain biking and white-water rafting (mainly spring for the latter, though rafting on the Oum er Rbia in the Middle Atlas is year-round). Your best starting point for such activities is Marrakesh. Details of organised adventures are often posted in budget and medium level hotels, such as Hotel Foucauld in Marrakesh and Grand Hôtel du Toubkal in Asni. There are also several tour operators specialising in adventure holidays in Morocco.

(tel: 048-248521). A new 9-hole complex has been built at **Beni Slimane** (tel: 023-297225) and the old 9-hole course at **Fez** (tel: 055-665210) is being improved and extended. Several new golf courses are scheduled; contact the Moroccan National Tourist Office or the Moroccan Golf Federation (tel: 037-755960).

Skiing

The most developed infrastructure is at Oukaimeden, 70 km (43 miles) from Marrakesh (season December to March), and simple facilities are found in Mischliffen, near Ifrane, south of Fez. Facilities (ski-lifts, pistes, accommodation) are rudimentary compared with those of European resorts. Cross-country skiing is more exhilarating.

For further details, contact the Federation Ski-Montagne, Parc de la Ligue Arabe, BP 15899, Casablanca, tel: 022-474979.

Hiking

Popular departure points for mountain adventures are Asni and Imlil, south of Marrakesh, where arrangements can be made for ascents of Mount Toubkal *(see page 61)*. Tours are led by guides, with porters and mules carrying the luggage. Basic accommodation is found in huts, local homes or tents.

Other good bases for hiking are Tabant and Oukaimeden in the Central High Atlas and, for more challenging hikes in the remote Jebel Siroua west of Ouarzazate, Talioune.

The Moroccan National Tourist Office publishes an annual booklet listing accred-

USEFUL ADDRESSES

Tourist Information Offices

Outside Morocco

London 205 Regent Street, London W1R 7DE; tel: 020-7437 0073; fax: 020-7734 8172
New York 20 East 46th Street #1201, New York 10017; tel 212 5572520; fax: 212 9498148.
Sydney 2/11 West Street, North Sydney, NSW 2060; tel: 9957 6717; fax: 99231053.
Montreal 1800 McGill College Avenue, Suite 2450, Montreal; tel: 842 8111; fax: 842 5316.

In Morocco

Agadir Avenue du Prince Heritier Sidi Mohammed (tel: 048-846377; fax: 048-846378) and Boulevard Mohammed V (tel: 048-840307).
Casablanca 55 Rue Omar Slaoui (tel: 022-271177; fax: 022-205929) and 98 Boulevard Mohammed V (tel: 022-221524).
Fez Place de la Résistance (tel: 055-941270; fax: 055-654370) and Place Mohammed V (tel: 055-654370).
Marrakesh Place Abdel Moumen Ben Ali, Boulevard Mohammed V (tel: 044-436239; fax: 044-436057).
Meknes 27 Place Administrative (tel: 055-524426; fax: 055-516046.
Rabat 22 Avenue al Jazair (Avenue d'Alger) (tel: 037-730562; fax: 037-727917).
Tangier 29 Boulevard Pasteur (tel: 039-948050; fax: 039-948661).

Above: outward bound

Embassies and Consulates
UK: 17 Boulevard de la Tour Hassan, Rabat
(tel: 037-238600).
USA: 13 Avenue Ahmed Balafrej, Souissi,
Rabat (tel: 037-758181).
Canada: 13 Bis Rue Jaafa Essadik BP 709,
Agdal, Rabat (tel: 037-687400).

Useful Websites
www.royalairmaroc.com
Royal Air Maroc's website; on-line booking.
www.gbairways.com
Website of GB Airways, which operates
flights from the UK to Agadir, Casablanca,
Marrakesh, Tangier and Fez .
www.tourism-in-morocco.com
The Moroccan National Tourist office online.
www.maroc.net
News and culture, plus useful information
www.oncf.org.ma
Information on the rail service in Morocco.
www.atlas-blue.com
Royal Air Maroc's low-cost flight site.
www.terremaroc.com
Tourist info site. Particularly good for finding *maison d'hotes* accommodation.

FURTHER READING

Insight Guide: Morocco (Apa Publications,
2002). In-depth history and essays as well as
comprehensive coverage of places.
Insight Compact Guide: Morocco (Apa Publications, 2002). Redesigned and expanded
with new maps and pictures.

History
Morocco That Was by Walter Harris. Eye-
witness account of the period leading to
the French Protectorate by the late 19th-
century Morocco correspondent of the
London *Times*.
Lords of the Atlas by Gavin Maxwell. Story
of the influential Glaoui dynasty that col-
laborated with the French.
The Conquest of Morocco by Douglas Porch.
A compelling history/saga of the French
takeover.

Travel
A Year In Marrakesh by Peter Mayne.
The Voices of Marrakesh by Elias Canetti.
Impressions by Nobel Prize winner.
Travels with a Tangerine by Tim Mackin-
tosh-Smith. Captivating account of a jour-
ney from Tangier to Istanbul in the footsteps
of a famous 14th-century Moroccan traveller.

Literary
The Spider's House by Paul Bowles. Set in
Fez during the period leading to independence, this is a gripping story of two American expatriates caught up in events.
The Sheltering Sky by Paul Bowles. Set in
the desert and exploring profound themes.
For Bread Alone by Mohamed Choukri. Powerful autobiography of a man who grew up
poor and illiterate around Tangier.
Tangier: City of the Dream by Iain Fin-
layson. Engrossing account of Tangier in its
louche heyday.
A Little Original Sin: The Life and Works of
Jane Bowles by Millicent Dillon. Biogra-
phy of Paul Bowles's writer wife, much of
which is concerned with her life in Tangier.

Art
Matisse in Morocco by Jack Cowart, Pierre
Schneider, John Elderfield, Alberct
Kostenevich and Laura Coyle. Lavish
record of Matisse's two fruitful visits to
Tangier in 1912.

Food and Cooking
Good Food from Morocco by Paula Wolfert.
Comprehensive and a diverting read.
Taste of Morocco by Robert Carrier. Recipes,
tips and insights, supported by sumptuous
photography.

Above: flags of state bearing Morocco's five-pointed star

www.insightguides.com

✳ INSIGHT GUIDES

The World Leader in Visual Travel Guides & Maps

As travellers become ever more discriminating, Insight Guides is using the vast experience gained over three-and-a-half decades of guide-book publishing to create an even wider range of titles to serve them. For those who want the big picture, Insight Guides and Insight City Guides provide comprehensive coverage of a destination. Insight Pocket Guides supply personal recommendations for a short stay. Insight Compact Guides are attractively portable. Insight FlexiMaps are both rugged and easy to use. And specialist titles cover shopping, eating out, and museums and galleries. Wherever you're going, our writers and photographers have already been there – more than once.

ACKNOWLEDGEMENTS

Photography	**Phil Wood** *except*
23T, 23B, 29, 31, 41T, 47, 49T, 52, 54T, 55B, 59, 70B, 74, 82, 86, 88	**Dominique Dallet**
13, 14B	**Alain le Garsmeur**
14T	**Hulton Getty**
2–3, 54B, 56T, 57, 58T, 65T, 66T	**Tony Halliday**
1, 16, 33, 42T, 60, 67, 69T, 70, 73, 75, 80, 83,	**Alan Keohane**
44	**Christine Osborne**
Cover	**Andrew Gunners/Digital Vision/ Getty Images**
Cartography	**Maria Randell**

© APA Publications GmbH & Co. Verlag KG Singapore Branch, Singapore

INDEX

Adventure after Cancer

My Walk

Land's End to John O'Groats

Kate Baker

Published in 2018 by Kate Baker

2nd Edition September 2018